WATERLOO
1815

Waterloo 1815

Ian Ribbons

Kestrel Books

KESTREL BOOKS
Published by Penguin Books Ltd
Harmondsworth, Middlesex, England

First published in 1982

ISBN 0 7226 5596 7

Filmset in Monophoto Times by
Northumberland Press Ltd, Gateshead
Printed in Great Britain by
Richard Clay (The Chaucer Press) Ltd,
Bungay, Suffolk

CONTENTS

Prelude

1

*S*UMMER *1815*

Since the spring there had been different travellers in the fast mails. Muffled in greatcoats against the night air or squeezed inside between farmer and squire, rich young men, silk shirts in their portmanteaux and diaries in their pockets, were too excited to sleep as their coaches sped through Rochester and Faversham on their way to the coast. For most of them, this was only the second summer in a lifetime that a holiday abroad was possible. In 1814 two decades of European war had finally ended, and with peace at last, English packets and sloops from the Channel ports were free to enter Ostend or Calais and to carry Continental traffic again.

Like the great East Indiamen moored in the port of London, which had always unloaded mail with their cargoes of spice, coastal shipping could now bring back news: not six months old from far-off Calcutta or China, but with its ink hardly *Portsmouth Harbour*

The Bank of England   dry. A letter written from Paris could, given dry roads and no
broken springs to the diligence, reach the coast within a week;
and, if luck produced a favourable wind, be cast ashore in its
mail bag on Dover pier within a day and a half more. Once
in England and locked in the boot of the scarlet Dover and
London Royal Mail, it could be at the Saracen's Head in
Friday Street in 11 hours, and its seals broken on a London
newspaper desk by the following breakfast.

In April, it had seemed, briefly, that all holiday plans might
be ruined. Newspapers were suddenly full of an astounding
story of rebellion in France, an army deserting its lawful king,
a new spectre of war. In England certain Militia units were
embodied, and in Portsmouth and Norwich and a score of

villages folk watched recruits at musket drill as regular army regiments were slowly brought up to strength.

But by May it seemed that perhaps the alert was a false alarm. Information dried up from France, and for tourists who felt that country unsafe there was plenty to see in Belgium and Holland. If the slippery Boney – the former Emperor, Napoleon Bonaparte – had indeed raised an army, the combined forces of Prussia, Russia, Austria and Britain would surely soon be strong enough to stamp out any trouble before it started. As the country carter left his week-old parcel of newspapers at the village inn, the rural doctor or parson who read them at leisure could feel it would all come to nothing.

Although England was, for perhaps the first time, proud of her army, at least of the small but disciplined band that had beaten the French out of the Spanish Peninsula, most people fell back into their usual habit of ignoring it. The common soldier was either a vagabond or a criminal who enlisted for drink – so opinion held – and every parish distrusted him. The tattered red-coats, disbanded as old or maimed from the last war, begging for bread in London's streets, were soon hustled away on paupers' carts, handcuffed if need be, from county to county and finally below decks to Ireland.

For the jobber or merchant perusing his *Morning Post* – or any of the fifteen London daily papers – in his accustomed chop house, his main interest that summer was money. Stocks for sale in foreign adventuring companies, shares in the new Regent's Canal then digging further towards Camden Town, houses building into the countryside north of the New Road from Paddington; and for his wife the last flurry of the London 'season'. The famous actor Edmund Kean was playing Shylock at Drury Lane, and every afternoon the 'fashionable promenade, unequalled for splendour' which the annual *Picture for London* praised, wound its way through Hyde Park and Kensington Gardens. Costume was simpler; Madame

Amaudrut advertised that she had 'arrived from Paris' with dresses 'in the newest style'. For evening receptions a plume of seven ostrich feathers and real pearls were the thing.

Costumes of the period

And there was music and art. Few visitors paying their shilling for the 47th Summer Exhibition at the Royal Academy at Somerset House might have noticed the eight landscapes, all unsold, by a certain John Constable; but one, of a barge being built near Flatford Mill – the first picture ever shown in the Royal Academy to have been painted entirely in the open air – was almost a reflection of England: a land still of

South view of Somerset House

trees and water, of workmen hewing timber. And as for books, it was the year Jane Austen finished *Emma*, who 'handsome, clever, and rich ... had lived nearly twenty-one years in the world with very little to distress or vex her'.

Millbank in 1815

By June it was almost as if everyone had forgotten the British battalions assembling in Belgium, although there were those near the coast who might have seen straws in the wind: the clerks at Miles and Minter's General Coach Office who remarked the string of rosy-cheeked youngsters, tight-buttoned in scarlet and awkward with swords, clambering down at the Canterbury staging post; and at the end of the route the ostlers at Ramsgate's Castle Tavern pocketing their tips, as senior officers handed them their horses for stabling before sailing ahead for their regiments. On Friday the 16th, watchers from Dover cliffs could have picked out the sails of a troop convoy making slowly up-Channel towards Deal and the Downs. Newspapers carried brief paragraphs. The *Kentish Gazette* reported another detachment of the Royal Waggon Train 'on their march from Croydon', and private carts hired at Chelmsford 'to carry one and a half million ball cartridges', and a further 30 million cartridges and 30,000 powder barrels embarked at Woolwich.

But inland, things remained normal. That day, the Duke of Norfolk and thirty other guests sat down to dinner at the start of a 'Grand Baronial Fête' at Arundel Castle lasting three days, devouring in a day – with the help of 200 servants – an ox, three sheep, three calves, and 'venison and sweetbreads in great profusion'. On Sunday, also announced the *Morning Post*, 'the divine Miss O'Neill', the actress, was to grace a

Covent Garden

midnight *conversazione*, or party, at Salisbury House. And as on all Fridays, more than 1,000 costermongers were preparing carts to drive in to early London markets, to sell food to London's poor. Through the small hours gangs of women from Isleworth's fruit gardens, with 'loades' of June strawberries on their heads, were tramping the silent countryside past Knightsbridge, approaching the boundary of town at Hyde Park Turnpike. Wherries were filled with asparagus from Battersea, ready to be rowed across the river, and sail barges packed with greens and lettuces were gliding downstream from Fulham. Along the Westminster and Strand wharves and up Southampton Street, faint flares like glow-worms lit the routes towards the great vegetable and fruit market of Covent Garden.

The tide was ebbing more slowly now; in little more than an hour it would be low water. Below London Bridge, along the mudflats beside the Dutch eel-boats lying at anchor, barefoot mudlarks, mostly orphan children, were scraping their precarious living from the river bed: bones and fragments of coal and nails they could sell for coppers. Upstream, close by the line of coster carts beginning to grind up Bridge Street from Blackfriars Bridge, new steam machinery in Printing House Square had been running the sheets of *The Times*'s first edition since 1.30 a.m.

The Southwark end of London Bridge

As always, its foreign news columns were full of rumour. Napoleon Bonaparte, or 'Boney', had apparently arrived at the headquarters of the rebel army. One report from Rotterdam, dated the 13th, put him 'at Mauberge'. Another claimed an attempt had been made on his life. But nothing definite. There had been no definite news of Bonaparte for weeks. For London it was just another Saturday.

While most of the city slept, the Thames ran silently, past the faint outlines of the Tower, past the close-moored merchantmen of the lower reaches, past the slipways of Deptford towards the widening estuary. The wind was stronger beyond the Nore, chopping low water off the sandbanks. Out to sea, still only some miles off Ramsgate, the fleet of troop transports was labouring close-hauled, making little way, beginning to scatter.

2

NIGHT AT QUATRE BRAS

Across the Channel lay the coast of Belgium, by Ostend. The night was paling; at 3.30 a low line of sand hills beside the sea glimmered light grey against dark. Fields behind were lost in darkness, but first hints of dawn revealed the black spires of churches. Southwards and eastwards the land stretched flat, field after field; then a long, straight canal; but after dense tree masses surrounding Brussels it rose south-eastwards again to a low plateau.

Under weak stars a breeze stirred a broad tract of bracken and patches of tall rye. Dim shapes of carts and men were moving slowly north-west from a crossroads; behind them guns, ammunition wagons, and long ranks of tethered horses lined the fields; the darkness of lower slopes hid crouching figures with muskets. In places the corn was flattened by things smooth and shiny: helmets, men with upturned faces, the bellies of horses. An occasional shot cut through the cries for water. This was part of an army in battle position, held after a bitter struggle; the name of the hamlet by the crossroads was Quatre Bras; the men were Dutch, Germans, some Belgians, but mostly British.

Southwards, beyond another line of pickets, Frenchmen were sleeping in their thousands. The Château of Fleurus, Napoleon's night headquarters, was guarded by standing cavalry and bearskinned sentries from the legendary Imperial Guard.

On the edges of the vast bivouacs of a French army lay the

smouldering ruins of another village, studded with dead, with smashed guns, littered equipment, stretching on both sides of Ligny stream. Northwards, more men were plodding open farmland. In growing light they could be seen, without rank, many without muskets, others lying by ditches. Their insignia were from three Prussian army corps. Their commander, Field Marshal von Blücher, a tough old man of seventy-three, lay bandaged in a tiny cottage at Mellery. His frail, bruised body was no longer young, but his iron will had already determined that his shattered army would stand to fight again.

Across country from Blücher the road from Quatre Bras ran north to Brussels, crossed the river Dyle and rose to the village of Genappe. By the inn sign of the King of Spain, a group of horsemen had gathered in the narrow street. The half-light barely distinguished colours of capes, cockades, lace, but was enough to define the ridged nose and slim figure, wrapped in a plain cloak, of one beginning to move off southwards. Talking stopped, harness clinked, and a file of some twenty riders clopped down the cobbles behind their leader.

He was Commander-in-Chief of a British and Netherlands army, born Arthur Wesley, his title now Field Marshal His Grace the Duke of Wellington.

3

*A*LARMS AND WAR

Just one year ago Wellington was dictating dispatches from Paris, Blücher was enjoying a triumphant visit to London, and Napoleon was pacing the hills of a Mediterranean prison. At long last, in the early summer of 1814, Napoleon's armies were finally defeated. Napoleon was forced to sign his abdication, and was allotted the tiny kingdom of Elba – with an English Governor as gaoler. The Bourbon claimant, Louis XVIII, was made King of France, and Wellington, leader of an undefeated army which had fought its way from Lisbon to the Pyrenees and become the talk of the world, transformed into British Ambassador. Paris, after years of isolation as capital of an embattled Empire, again throbbed with fashionable visitors from London, Vienna, Russia. Once again the Grand Tour became possible, and while people of leisure travelled the dusty south, the diplomats of ten nations assembled in Vienna for a Congress to redraw Europe's frontiers, to rebalance powers as a buttress to peace.

Elba

Blücher bade a reluctant farewell to the speeches and kisses of England and retired to Silesia; and the British government, fearing Wellington's safety amidst anti-British agitation in Paris, sent him to negotiate for Britain at Vienna. Even with his energy, a Congress bogged between secret intrigue and frivolous entertainment was still crawling painfully forward in the following spring when, on 7 March, a letter from Florence dropped the bombshell.

Napoleon, the elusive Ogre, had escaped.

Events moved fast. All delegates were united now in one sentiment, that a man who would tear up any treaty could never again be trusted. Stung by the spectre of revolution, and new wars, the Congress proclaimed Napoleon 'beyond the Law', subject to 'public justice': but the man himself, not France, the enemy. Wellington would command an Allied army to be raised in Flanders; Britain was to supply money, and troops to join with the Dutch–Belgian forces of the new King of the Netherlands. Aged though he was, Blücher was called to put his glamour and prestige once more at the head of a Prussian army to act with the Allies; Austria and Russia would ultimately march 350,000 men across Germany and into France from the east.

Napoleon, meanwhile, had judged his time. Landing with a mere 1,200 men in the Golfe Juan, he moved steadily north. First at Grenoble, then at Lyons, regiments sent to stop him simply threw away their Bourbon colours and flocked to his flag. Officers and men came in from all sides. Louis fled to Ghent, and within twenty days of landing on French soil Napoleon was in Paris, without a shot having been fired against him.

To veterans who had conquered Europe under the Imperial Eagle, the humiliation of defeat, the smouldering resentment towards a bloated Bourbon king, were suddenly over. Triumphant that their 'saviour' had indeed returned, they were ready to follow him to the ends of the earth.

Napoleon in fact may well have desired peace, but already hostile forces menaced his frontiers. It had to be war, or surrender. At full speed, with all his energy, he set about creating a new *Grande Armée* from the remnants of the old.

Wellington reached Brussels on 5 April. The next day he wrote expressing his disgust to the Secretary for War. 'It appears to me that you have not taken in England a clear view of your situation ... You have not called out the militia ... and how we are to make out 150,000 men ... appears not to have been considered ... we are in a bad way.'

He did not exaggerate. A mixed Anglo-Dutch contingent contained only 14,000 British troops. The bulk of Wellington's superb Peninsular Army was either at sea, returning from a useless American war, or disbanded. Belgium was largely pro-French; Belgian troops either recruits, or veterans who had fought for Napoleon and were liable to desert at the first chance. The Prince of Orange, an inexperienced twenty-two-year-old, although agreeing to surrender overall army command, was thrust on Wellington as a full Corps Commander. His brother of eighteen likewise. Border fortresses were in ruin. Supplies and equipment, when eventually prised out of a bumbling administration in London, had to come in by treacherous open harbour at Ostend or by long voyage via Antwerp. Some generals, particularly of cavalry, had been sent out to him against his wishes. The Whig opposition party in England was against war, anyway. And time was running out.

Incessant work, however, produced the near miracle of order. Although as late as 8 May Wellington was confiding to a friend, 'I have got an infamous army, very weak ...,' by May's end it was growing in strength, and spread in cantonments across north Belgium. South-east of the Bavay–Maastricht road stretched four Prussian army corps, their outposts joining Allied at Binche. At Tirlemont, Wellington and Blücher had met and agreed to act together, and to pass information freely by a liaison officer in each H.Q. Wellington's H.Q. remained in Brussels, together with a reserve corps under his direct command. His two other corps he pushed forward, dispersed east and west with cavalry between, and a cavalry screen south of all in observation. Should Blücher be attacked, Wellington agreed to concentrate the bulk of his force around Nivelles.

But if Napoleon were to move first, before the Austrians and Russians could join a great Allied offensive in the summer, he could come by any of three possible roads. Firstly, against the Prussians through Charleroi; secondly, towards Brussels through Mons; or thirdly, towards Ghent and the Channel via

Tournai, thereby threatening the precarious line of supply from Ostend. Wellington's vital brief was to hold Brussels, but his army's life depended on its supplies. He was forced therefore to keep his divisions spread wide. Before launching them on anything up to a two days' march across country to concentrate against an attack, it was vital to be certain they were not being drawn aside by a feint, leaving Brussels open to capture by a lightning stroke along another route. Napoleon was past master at such a move.

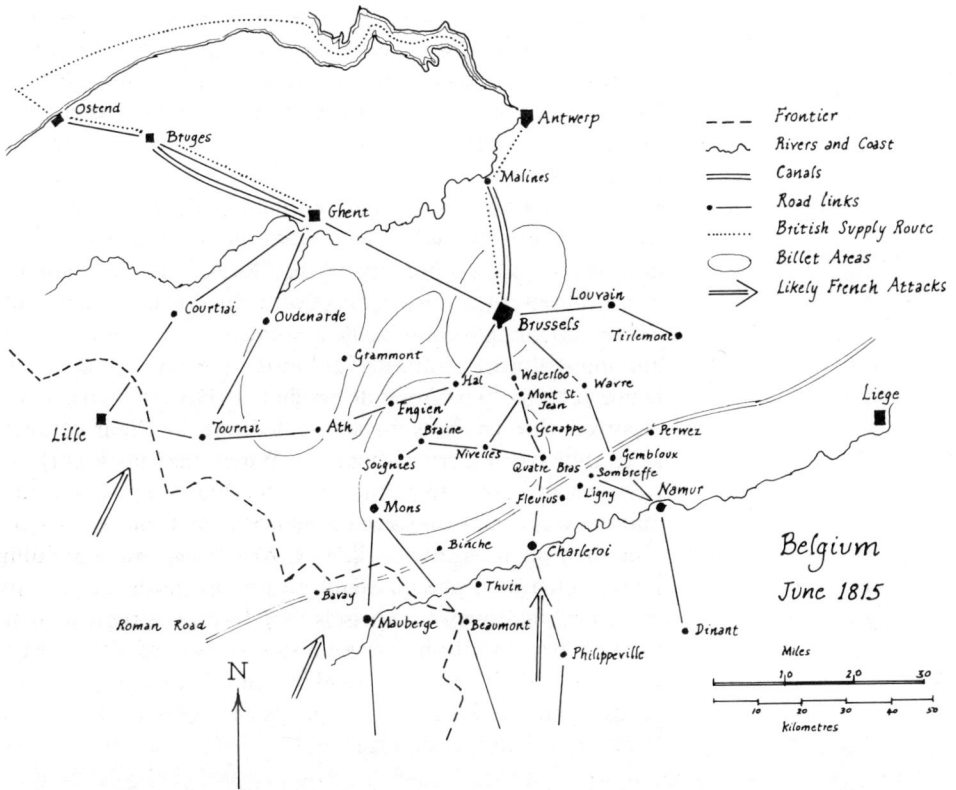

During May all reports from spies agreed that French troops were massing behind the frontier, but exactly where, and whether Napoleon was with them or still in Paris, remained a mystery. By 13 June, Wellington was actually writing, 'I think we are too strong for him here.'

Then, on Thursday the 15th, delayed dispatches broke the news that Prussian outposts had been driven in at Thuin, and alarm guns heard along the Sambre. With no information from his advanced cavalry, Wellington refused Blücher's request to shift his army immediately to Nivelles, but did warn all units

to gather on assembly points within their areas. It was still possible that the real attack would come through Mons. When, towards 10 p.m., Wellington at last heard that all French troops had indeed slipped east, towards the Prussians, he issued after-orders instructing units to march 'with as little delay as possible' towards Nivelles.

The situation was serious, but not unduly worrying, and with no more immediately to be done Wellington went at midnight to a ball put on by the Duchess of Richmond. It was a glittering affair, packed with fashionable society and with many of his own officers, already under marching orders, making the most of a last night in the capital. As supper was being served, two more dispatches arrived; Prussians were reported thrown back in severe fighting at Fleurus; and a separate French force was in contact with the Dutch at Quatre Bras, on the main Brussels road. The Dutch divisional commander was rushing a second brigade there in support.

A map in the house spelled out the danger with appalling clarity. Quatre Bras lay twenty-five miles inside the frontier, more than half-way to Brussels itself. And the nearest British division was twenty-five miles away westwards, others as far off again, as far west as Oudenaarde. Wellington's reserve corps around Brussels was in fact as near Quatre Bras as any. It would be a desperate race.

Wellington remained at the ball only long enough to avoid any appearance of panic. Immediately his H.Q. began working through the night drafting further route orders: everyone to press on beyond Nivelles towards Quatre Bras; V Division to march from Brussels by dawn and make for a road fork at Mont St Jean.

Early that Friday morning, long before light tipped the roofs of the city, drums beat troops from their billets; officers, with and without baggage, were rounded up by orderlies; and regiments began assembling in the Park. Soon after 3 a.m., columns of infantry, Scottish regiments with pipes wailing, began marching out from the Namur Gate. Wellington snatched three hours' sleep, was up by 5 a.m., and by 7 was riding with his staff on the Genappe road.

Threading the dusty files of marching infantry, he reached Quatre Bras at 10 a.m. to find only French pickets visible and everything quiet. Dispatch riders were sent to hurry on all troops at top speed through Nivelles, and also to bring on V Division beyond the road fork, but none could be expected for at least three hours. While waiting, Wellington rode by a cross road seven miles to Ligny, to meet the astonishing sight of a whole Prussian army in position and facing imminent attack. From a windmill, Wellington and Blücher could even make out with their telescopes a distant, single figure on horseback: Napoleon, apparently himself marshalling the massive blue lines of the French.

At last Wellington learned the truth: Napoleon had crossed the Sambre two nights before and his whole Imperial Army was on the move. It was a breakdown in Prussian information links that had kept him in the dark.

The Prussian Chief of Staff argued again for immediate support, and Wellington eventually agreed that once his army was concentrated around Quatre Bras, and provided he was not attacked before, he would move across to join Blücher. By 3 p.m. he was back at the crossroads; but by then the prospect had vastly changed. French columns were already forming.

All through the afternoon two distinct battles grew in intensity while smoke thickened under the crying birds. Again and again French columns and guns smashed into the Prussians, Blücher fell and was ridden over in a cavalry charge, men died in thousands, but by evening the Prussians broke, and Napoleon gained the ruins of Ligny. Other French infantry and cavalry made charge after charge before the crossroads of Quatre Bras and amid the farmland southward. The British V Division marched up in bare time to throw out a defence screen along the Ligny road; Guards regiments doubling and gasping the last mile from Nivelles charged a wood; time and again Wellington's line seemed almost broken, only to be saved by new reinforcements coming up from west and north. By nightfall the Anglo-Dutch were still in position, and the French pulled away south.

As Wellington rode back to Genappe for food and sleep the sound of battle away to the east by Ligny was dying down. The last message from Blücher to reach him, about 6 p.m., had said that he could hold on till night; Wellington could only suppose the Prussians were still in position too.

During the hours of darkness two men took fateful decisions. Count von Gneisenau, Prussian Chief of Staff, with only a thin rearguard facing the enemy, knew his army had to regroup well to the rear; but whether east towards Liège, which would be safer, or northward and parallel to Wellington's road to Brussels, was debated at length. Gneisenau distrusted Wellington. For all he knew, the British might go right back through Ghent and sail for England, leaving Belgium to its fate. Certainly, not a single British soldier had marched across to help stem the disaster at Ligny. Eventually he decided on Wavre, eighteen miles north, but still open to retreat east if finally necessary. When Blücher was discovered in Mellery, belligerent as ever, he emphatically agreed: 'We've had a dent and must straighten it out.' The march would begin in the early morning.

The real key, and second decision, was in the hands of Napoleon. So far he had made the running. A surprise crossing of the Sambre had been followed by an immediate advance in two wings: the left, under Marshal Ney – who had rejoined the army that same day – was still blocked at Quatre Bras, but the right, under his own command, had gained certain victory at Ligny. With the bulk of his whole force now able to concentrate against Quatre Bras, the result could never be in doubt.

Tomorrow the Anglo-Dutch would be swept aside like flies, or crushed. A 'Proclamation to the Belgians', dated in advance for the 17th, lay ready in his carriage: '... the God of Battles has decided ... Napoleon is among you ... your enemies ... fly with rage and despair ...' By the 18th he would be in Brussels, the Belgians would rise against the Dutch, and he would have won a resounding victory before the Prussians or anyone else could raise a finger.

Meanwhile there seemed no need to rush. His troops badly needed rest, and since the enemy was clearly routed and helpless all pursuit was halted for the night, to await reorganization in the morning.

The French simply went into bivouac.

Saturday 17 June 1815

4

𝒫LANS

Now through the chilly mist of early morning Wellington was riding back at 4 a.m. to Quatre Bras. His erect, neat figure showed no strain from only seven hours' sleep in two nights: spartan habits and a lifetime in the saddle had left him, at forty-six, still in the peak of condition.

Wellington was not born to soldiering; his first talent was for music. But at seventeen, the middle son of an aristocratic but none too wealthy family, he was bundled off to Angers Academy in Anjou to learn horsemanship, French, fencing and mathematics as a gateway to an army career. He set himself to becoming a complete professional: turning his back on an apparently hopeless love, he burnt his violin and read every authority he could find on war, strategy and organization.

In 1794 in Flanders, during one of the first campaigns of the Napoleonic war, he learned an undying lesson: that winter nearly a third of a starving expeditionary force froze to death on the north Dutch plains from lack of supplies. Later, as a young general in India, he won a string of victories based on daring manoeuvre and sudden, precisely timed attack. In the Peninsula of Spain and Portugal he had to evolve new tactics of defence against repeatedly larger enemies, to stretch invariably inadequate resources to the last mule or bullet, to forge an efficient command system from nothing, to suffer unpredictable allies; but in the end beating every Marshal that Napoleon could send against him. Often cold in manner, hiding the disappointment of a marriage gone sour, ruthlessly critical of laziness or incompetence yet never expecting more than was reasonable, he spared himself less than anyone. As campaign followed campaign through the breadth of a barren Peninsula, he built a superb army. His men gave him not so much their affection as complete confidence and loyalty. 'Here he comes with his long nose, boys, you may fix your flints,' an Irish brogue would call, as the familiar figure appeared among the lines. With 'Old Nosey to command' they were 'sure to give the enemy a damn good thrashing. What can a soldier desire more?' To most of Europe, dazzled by his success, he was simply 'the Duke'.

Impassive, apparently serene, inwardly he anxiously weighed probabilities. Yesterday he was as near defeat as he'd ever been in his life. Forced then to defend a featureless position in order to keep the vital cross route open to the Prussians, he was today still with only part of his army concentrated, many units still to march up. And he was holding ground far too exposed for safety.

Things seemed suspiciously quiet. No smoke from enemy camp-fires might mean the French had retreated. Wellington's movements, once his troops were gathered, depended on Blücher's; properly combined, the two armies would be strong enough to take the offensive, but it was ten hours since any message. A British night patrol had reported only French near the Ligny road; it was vital to have fresh news.

Wellington sent off a senior aide-de-camp, Colonel Gordon, with a cavalry troop from 10th Hussars to find out what had happened, and while awaiting their return walked over to nearby bivouacs of 92nd, Gordon Highlanders. Only half its numbers rallied to Piper Cameron's call last night; the rest lay heaped by a farmhouse hedge, killed or wounded in a furious charge. The men were unusually silent and depressed.

Wellington dismounted briskly. '92nd, I will be obliged to you for a little fire.' Brawny Highlanders soon had a blaze crackling outside a ruined log hut, while others dragged up branches and twigs to plug its gaping walls. After their commander and senior staff had set up temporary headquarters inside, the soldiers stood around the fire; their sodden kilts steaming in the warmth. Along the damp fields soldiers were bestirring themselves, seeking water, thinking of food, looking to equipment, preparing for another day's labours.

One grim task was to dig burial pits for 'all the dead bodies within our reach, especially the officers', wrote Sgt Robertson of the 92nd. Many soldiers were still lying untended between skirmish lines. Lt George Simmons, going back with one company from the 95th Rifles, found 'among some bushes ... a pair of legs booted and spurred' and hauled out a French cavalry officer. Unbuckling the cuirass from the man's chest, he discovered the body still breathing. He ordered two lightly wounded from a bed inside a farmhouse for the Frenchman,

and returned to increasing musketry and a growing number of blue specks gathering in the cornfields opposite. Among them, silhouetted against the morning mist, some mounted officers were coolly surveying the Allied lines.

Simmons, a stocky Yorkshireman, was something of a joker. To cheer his men he dressed up in the cuirass and huge gloves and paraded up and down amid laughter, mocking the French. 'It was not wide enough for my brawny shoulders, but much too long ... Johnny took it as an insult. I had 3 or 4 shots knocking up the dust pretty near me, which I returned. The farmer came to see the fun ...' His sergeant got a ball in the arm; growling, 'the game is up with me for this campaign anyhow,' he begged a last shot at the French. Simmons let him lay his rifle 'over my left shoulder, and with his left hand ... took deliberate aim and fired'. Satisfied, the veteran hobbled back to the surgeons.

Inside Wellington's staff hut, minutes, an hour, dragged by without news of Blücher. Until it came, Wellington could decide nothing. Dawn had brought no enemy move, and although a strong line of French skirmishers was busy exchanging shots with his outlying pickets, their level of fire did not suggest imminent attack. However, Napoleon's armies had always lived off the land, and in this half-ravaged countryside no mass of men could sit still for long. The French must either

retreat – which under Napoleon was unlikely – slip away and try to outflank, or reform quickly and come head on. If present firing was simply to cover a withdrawal, the sooner he and Blücher joined forces and pressed south the better.

Suddenly, at 7 a.m., a movement on the Ligny road. Col. Gordon, Wellington's aide-de-camp (A.D.C.), was riding back fast at the head of his escort and was immediately directed to Wellington's hut. After only some minutes the Duke joined waiting staff officers outside. One Guards officer, Capt. Bowles, a personal friend of Wellington, was watching from a little distance. The Duke seemed to be speaking quietly, but urgently. Some officers immediately left, and then Wellington walked quickly across to speak to Bowles. The news was astounding. Gordon had found no Prussian troops at all, except for a rearguard; Ligny was abandoned. 'Old Blücher has had a damned good licking and gone back to Wavre ...' Before Bowles could reply, Wellington continued, as if to himself, 'I suppose in England they will say we have been licked. I can't help it; as they are gone back, we must go too.' He stayed only a moment; as more staff rode away with warning orders, he re-entered the hut with senior officers to prepare detailed route plans.

Among those inside were Col. Delancey, the thirty-four-year-old American Deputy Quartermaster General who had already distinguished himself while serving under Wellington in Spain; Gordon and other staff; and General Baron Muffling, the Prussian liaison officer at British H.Q. Wellington glowered at Muffling: a whole Prussian army had apparently decamped without a word, leaving the British high and dry. Muffling stressed that he also had heard nothing since last night; he could only think Prussian dispatch riders had been cut down or captured on the road. He had to explain that things were even worse than the others realized. Wavre, which no one could find on the map, was fully eighteen miles north of Ligny.

Already the news was spreading gloom through the 92nd and other nearby regiments. To a soldier, retreat now simply meant that men had given their lives yesterday in vain. Some generals felt the same. General Sir Thomas Picton, the crusty commander of V Division, gave Basil Jackson a 'surly acknowledgement' when the young A.D.C. delivered the order. Col. Frazer, commanding Royal Horse Artillery, began a hasty letter home:

'Quatre Bras, June 17, half-past 7 a.m.

... we shall retrograde a little, and I have sent off the ammunition carriages of the horse artillery to the forest of Soignes, near Waterloo ... The action now seems recommencing.'

As the rattle of skirmish fire rose and fell, Wellington, hiding anger or bitterness, discussed timings. His whole army was tired and hungry; must men undertake another long march on empty stomachs? Muffling thought not, pointing out that the French had bivouacked late last evening, and in such cases 'it was always Napoleon's custom, in his wars in Germany, to allow his troops first to cook, and to break up at ten the next morning'. Wellington took a calculated risk that full-scale attack was unlikely for some hours, and ordered supply wagons to unload.

Leaving Delancey to write out movement details, the Duke went outside, where one of the 92nd's officers, Lt Hope, watched him for a whole hour, pacing up and down alone. Worries about Blücher, about Napoleon's next move and, above all, about the danger of a long retreat by narrow roads to which his own army would be exposed, showed only in certain mannerisms. The fascinated Hope noticed 'a small switch in his right hand, the one end of which he frequently put to his mouth ... His left hand was thrown carelessly behind his back ...' His pace was fast, '$3\frac{1}{2}$–4 miles in the hour'.

Fires were crackling in the hedges by now. Among the 95th Rifles, Simmons was lucky; a farm had food for sale. He stripped off his cuirass to make a fry-pan; in no time eggs and 'skinned fowls and bacon were hissing and spluttering upon it in gravy'. His commanding officer, Sir Andrew Barnard, with a general in tow, was drawn by the smell and given first pick. Barnard wiped his mouth cheerfully. 'Now let the French come on, as soon as they like ...' The general began to apologize for holding up Simmons, but Barnard cut him short: 'he is fully capable of taking care of himself ... George, you had better look sharp ...', and squatting beside them George tucked in too. The farmer even produced wine, at 1s. a bottle.

The new style cooking spread fast. Another ravenous young lieutenant, John Black, making up for dry biscuit, wrote later to his father: 'well in a minnet a bull was driven in to the Regiment, killed, we got some cuirasses which made the best

frying pans in the World … so you may not talk of beef
hanging for a week before it is good … the beef was alive ten
minutes before you eat it.'

All men were fiercely hungry. Capt. Cavalié Mercer, Royal
Horse Artillery, was alarmed by a crowd of red-coats streaming
towards his troop of guns as if in sudden retreat, then saw
cheering men clubbing, bayoneting, axing a running pig. On
cavalry outpost, Capt. Grove found that his regiment, 23rd
Light Dragoons, had only 'something like a very old cow' still
'smoking with its natural heat'. Grove was as brave as any,
but the animal had him beaten; he left it untouched.

5

THE MARCH UP

Cavalry and artillery were still coming in to strengthen the British and Dutch at Quatre Bras when, soon after 9 a.m., a dusty cavalry officer rode up with the long-awaited word from Blücher himself. The Prussians had indeed regrouped at Wavre. The officer could speak English, and was questioned closely by Wellington. At length the Duke made a formal declaration to Muffling, as Blücher's representative, that he 'would accept a battle in the position of Mont St Jean, if the Field-Marshal were inclined to come to his assistance even with one corps only'. As the Prussian officer rode away with this message, routes and timings for the move had already been prepared by Delancey and his staff. All generals and commanding officers were summoned. 'On my arrival I found by the questions of the Duke and Lord Uxbridge who were looking over a map that we were about to retreat ...' wrote Lt-Col. Dalrymple of 15th Hussars.

One vital map had been nearly lost. Engineers in April had
surveyed a long ridge south of Waterloo village, the more
northerly of two which cut the Brussels road between there and
Genappe, and staff officers had marked the position as the best
defence line available before the capital. One map copy was
with the Prince of Orange; the other, brought from Brussels
yesterday by an Engineer, Lt Waters, had only been recovered
this morning from the 'cloak before his saddle' when his horse
was found 'grazing on the vegetables in a garden', after becoming trapped in a cavalry charge during yesterday's battle.
Waters escaped, terrified the plan had fallen into enemy hands.
His nightmare over, he saw his Brigade-Major thankfully hand
it over to be passed to Delancey.

Col. Frazer, commanding Royal Horse Artillery, was continuing his letter home: '... half-past 9. Preparations making
for withdrawing ... We are sending off spare carriages, etc. etc.
The chef d'etat major of a French division deserted to us last
night, bringing returns of the French force, which amounts to
130,000 ... An officer has just come from Blücher to the Duke.'

Except for the picket line, most soldiers had swallowed what
food they could get, and now had little to do before the move.
'Our men employed in rummaging the dead Frenchmen and we
in reading their letters and memorandums ... occasionally interrupted by a few stray shots,' noted a seventeen-year-old
Ensign, Edward Macready, with 2/30th Foot. Mercer, the
seasoned professional, with one of the smartest troops in the
Horse Artillery, was assessing whether his guns would be
needed or not: 'a smart skirmish was going on amongst the
hedges ... Our infantry were lying about, cleaning their arms,
cooking, or amusing themselves, totally regardless ... I saw

French tirailleurs suddenly make a rush ... The fire then again became sharper than ever, but the French were driven back.'

Frequently Wellington had his telescope up. Until all baggage and ammunition wagons and convoys of wounded were safely away the infantry could not march. Fortunately, still no sign of a real attack.

Almost more urgency in rear areas; to north and east long dust clouds marked the line of other brigades moving up to join the army. Furthest away was General Lambert's, which got orders in Ghent, marched thirty long miles yesterday towards Brussels, slept by the road, and with packs hoisted at dawn began another day-long tramp today. As they reached the city's outskirts, a staff officer from Delancey met the head of column, bringing orders to make for Quatre Bras and not Nivelles.

A column on the march had strange additions. The Brigade-Major, Harry Smith, a dapper twenty-eight-year-old, was riding with his young Spanish bride. He had found her, only fourteen at the time, sheltering in the ruins of Badajoz; married her; and had scarcely had her out of his sight since. She kept his tent through the bitter winters of the Pyrenees, rode with the troops through a whole campaign, and was now almost a mascot. At one time Smith had thirteen dogs and greyhounds and one destitute priest in his entourage.

The sun was climbing higher in the sky; yesterday some men in the Guards brigade actually fell dead with heat. Field service marching order was no joke: half throttled in leather stock or stiff collar, an infantryman was strapped and harnessed under knapsack, greatcoat, blankets, canteen for water and kettle for cooking, haversack with three days' biscuit or bread, musket and 120 rounds of ball cartridge – more than 60 lb. of load. Marching in column of route, four abreast, soldiers were allowed to break step, falling out for a few minutes' rest each hour. Lambert's Peninsular veterans, uniforms patched and stained, had landed nine days ago in Ostend direct from the American war, without setting foot in England. The artist Benjamin Robert Haydon heard about the infamous Inniskillings, the 1/27th, from a wounded rifleman last winter. 'He said one Irish regiment took off all their buttons, and passed them for shillings. They had changed clothes so often with the dead, enemies and English, that, on meeting the Duke once, he did not know what regiment they were.'

A clop of hooves, the order 'Open right and left', and to universal 'hissing, hooting and yelling' a hated cavalcade passed towards the front: 'mounted on a grey pony, a hideous-looking man with an enormous head, a pale pasty complexion, small cunning grey eyes', with a cocked hat and silk sash, half a dozen drummers holding to his pony by straps, carrying drum cases full of whips and greased ropes 'with nooses all ready for immediate use'. The words are those of George Keppel, a sixteen-year-old Ensign with the 3/14th; the man a Provost Marshal, each division's agent of rough discipline for a rough army. Looting, murder, desertion, sleeping on sentry duty, striking an officer: all carried sentence of death. Lesser offences up to 400 lashes.

6

$\mathcal{B}$OATS, HORSES, SUPPLIES

A small man with unbuttoned coat was riding slowly across Ligny battlefield. By his side a Marshal of the Army, close behind a group of senior officers. Napoleon had been up and about for four hours, but after yesterday's violent action seemed unusually lethargic. At 8 a.m. he sent vague orders to Ney at Frasnes, to probe Quatre Bras; if found to be lightly defended take it; otherwise the day to be spent consolidating and bringing up stragglers. Napoleon had had Ney's reply that the British and the Dutch were in force; to attack, Ney would need far more troops; but so far, he had made no response. Marshal Grouchy reported three hours ago; instead of orders he was given a tour of Ligny. At 9 a.m., news of Prussians at Gembloux, north-east, and of a captured battery on the Namur road, suggested they were safely retreating east.

At last, at 11 a.m., Napoleon made up his mind. Ney was to attack forthwith, and would get 30,000 men in support, led by the Emperor himself. Grouchy was to move on Gembloux, from there to reconnoitre eastwards towards Namur and Maastricht; to find the enemy and pursue him. No one had reported that the Prussians had left hours ago, and were moving north, not east.

In a daring campaign two vital mistakes already: orders late, and orders confused. Now a third: long delays in carrying them out . . .

Another staff group was studying other ground. Delancey, half a mile south of Mont St Jean village, was marking out future troop positions, noting reference points on a sketch map for the new defence line after withdrawal from Quatre Bras. One thing already decided: no trenches would break the skyline of the low ridge; Wellington liked his main defences both flexible and secret. Although one company of sappers was on the move: the village of Braine l'Alleud was 'to be entrenched and made defensible' as a right-flank bastion to the position.

Main retreat road up to Mont St Jean still blocked. Lt Edmund Wheatley, a young Londoner with thirteen of his men from the 5th Line Battalion, King's German Legion, had been ordered up from Army H.Q. 'to clear the high road of all carts and carriages as far as Brussels and to suffer nothing but Artillery to come up'. He found Genappe's narrow streets 'choked up with wounded, and crowds and crowds of cavalry . . . each man leading his horse by the bridle with a wounded foot soldier laying across the saddle'. Against violent protests, his men put the commissary carts to use, tipping beef and gin into the ditches and loading them with wounded. Before he saw Wheatley's insignia a Brunswick sergeant of the escort galloped up swinging a pike: 'had I not parried with my sword he would have laid my skull open.'

One young officer on the D.Q.M.G. staff, Basil Jackson, couldn't get through even by using the flat of his sword and had to take to the fields. Before he could reach Mont St Jean he met his Chief, Delancey, coming back. With areas marked and guides left, work on the ridge was for the moment finished; Delancey told him to help clear the road. Wheatley was bellowing out orders when 'Commissary Beverly . . . gallop'd up . . . "Oh, Wheatley. How are ye? What think you of this mare? 150

guinea touch."' Spattered by the horse's hooves, hat and bread ration knocked in the mud, Wheatley told him savagely to get out: 'I'll examine your mare at a more convenient season.'

All the way from Genappe through to Brussels the paved highway was increasingly filled with carts, walking wounded, refugees with barrows and bundles, all moving north. Off the borders of the road, the gloomy forest of Soignes, where scarred beech glades marked the main timber supply for Napoleon's navies, hid wandering cattle, riderless horses, more wounded, officers in hired carriages.

In the Belgian capital normal life was at a standstill. All Friday afternoon crowds lining the ramparts had caught the faint booming of cannon borne on the wind, and when the first wounded arrived during the night, alarm and rumour spread fast. At midnight, allied artillery had been heard rumbling southwards towards the front, but at dawn a Belgian cavalry regiment had galloped in, crying all was lost, causing fresh panic.

This morning the streets seemed half-deserted, shops shuttered, visitors packing their bags. Most Belgians didn't care one way or the other – they had been part of the old French empire

for years – but British and other foreigners were aghast at the thought of a Napoleonic occupation. Inn yards were pandemonium, spare carriages like gold. One eye-witness saw people suddenly desperate to get away paying 'enormous sums' even for 'dog and fish carts'. Heavy furniture which couldn't be carried was being auctioned off, 'a chest of drawers sold for five francs, a bed for ten . . .' Madame D'Arblay, an Englishwoman better known as the novelist Fanny Burney, had been ten times to a friend for news, and was now arguing tearfully with the Military Commandant for a new passport. The fire-eating Colonel Jones would only stamp her old one, growling simply, 'It was not for *us*, the English, to spread alarm . . . he had not sent away his own wife and children.'

Unknown to most, the canal route to Antwerp was already closed, with all barges in the city basins commandeered for the army. In Antwerp itself, awaiting later use, the most massive material for Wellington's army lined the deep-water wharves: a complete bridging or pontoon train of forty specially built boat hulls strapped on top of special carts, with other carts for planking, ready for transport by barge. And a whole siege train disembarked from England: 526 wagons with over 1,000 horses; 83 huge Flanders wagons each with four draught horses; 700 other horses; 18 siege guns of 8-inch and 10-inch calibre and 140 mortars, howitzers and 18 and 24 pdr guns, all with full ammunition; all stood ready for the methodical pounding of French border fortresses when the summer's advance would begin.

Westwards, a freshening wind was blowing the spray from the tops of long breakers far out on the Ostend shore. Wellington's men knew Ostend: beaching in tossing row boats; troopers swinging out horses on rope shackles, to lower them from derricks into foaming surf; gun barrels choked, powder ruined; everyone drenched to the skin. Sometimes a complete ship swept by the strong current right past the narrow harbour entrance to run aground and break up on the sands. Disembarking was either a lark or a nightmare, according to one's responsibilities.

In mid-Channel, the fleet of seventeen troop transports had at last got under way when the wind veered at 5 a.m., and was speeding along with canvas booming 'at about 8 knots', according to Ensign Bakewell. Reinforcements from three companies of the 27th Inniskilling Fusiliers had returned twelve days ago from America. They would be with their naval escorts, *Sharpshooter* and *Snap* gun brigs, off Ostend by nightfall, together with some drafts from the reserve battalion, the whole 1st Battalion of the 7th Fusiliers, the 43rd Regiment, and large numbers of horses.

Across the Straits, Ramsgate had had a military air all week. Today, not troop transports but wide colliers for the wagon

*Transport off
North Foreland*

*Ramsgate from the
East Pier Head*

*View of Royal Naval
Hospital, Greenwich*

train were tied up alongside East Pier; Captain Ravenscroft, commanding the train, had come in ahead yesterday to supervise embarkation; the wagons were due in during the afternoon. Several officers, like Brevet-Major Thomas of the 1/27th, were awaiting sailing places to be arranged by the Transport Agent, others still arriving.

Coaches returning to London carried mostly civilians: the fast light coach *Wellington*, which rolled out from Goldsmid Place at 8 a.m., was by now an hour's run beyond Canterbury. Ahead the level road eventually rose to Shooter's Hill, from where the traveller would catch his first sight of the smoke haze of London. On a fine day, only the gleam of St Paul's dome showed above the perpetual cloud of coal soot, a shining landmark beyond the cupolas of Greenwich hospital and the line of the Thames.

View of St Paul's

Blocking the alleys and lanes of the City, huge brewers' drays – looking 'like elephants' to one American – carts and wagons and hackney coaches, messengers and clerks were clamouring through a usual Saturday workday. Civil servants like Charles Lamb – yet to achieve fame with his *Essays of Elia* – in East India House, inscribing the cost of 'indigoes, cottons, raw silks'; mail bags for Tuesday's monthly sailing to the Mediterranean being sorted in Sherborne Lane; in St Paul's churchyard the blind sailor fresh today out of Bridewell gaol – a week ago the beadle arresting him had two teeth knocked out by a crowd who sympathized with beggars. For visitors, the lame Indian tiger at the Tower zoo, or perhaps a guided tour, fifteen at a time, of the stuffed birds at the British Museum. Day trips to Gravesend had already slipped with the tide from Dice Quay, where ashore the smell of fish heads was all that was left of the early morning's Billingsgate market. And more significant than anything, the miles of masts of the massed shipping that used London, the biggest port in the world. Britain registered £35 millions of imports and £60 millions of exports that year.

Far from the noise of the City, Government offices in White-hall were also at work. Major-General Torrens had been at his desk in Horse Guards almost all week, writing, dictating, with little time to admire the vista of St James's Park before his windows. Torrens had carried a bullet in his thigh for sixteen

Billingsgate market from the river

Horse Guards from St James's Park

years past, had served in the West Indies, Canada, Spain and Egypt, but now as Military Secretary to the Commander-in-Chief, the Duke of York, his war was with red tape. The only letter today to Wellington's headquarters was a personal one; could Lord Fitzroy Somerset find a temporary job for a friend, a Colonel D'Aguilar of the Greek Light Infantry, who wanted to spend three months' leave 'as an amateur with the Army in Flanders'? Another letter recommended John Carrol, an old soldier, for a pension; another, signed by his secretary, pointed out that the unfortunate Ensign Hubbard, whose 'habitual drunkenness' had brought on a state of 'mental derangement' and was due to be 'removed from the service', was nevertheless owed more than a year's back pay.

Horse Guards

Almost nothing important could be done at first hand. 'I am directed by His Royal Highness the Commander-in-Chief to suggest to the favourable consideration of Earl Bathurst ...' runs every appeal to the Under-Secretary of State for War. To bring the Royal Waggon Train up to strength, Torrens reported today, each of the twelve troops needed farriers, collar-makers, wheelwrights, as well as officers and '130 privates and 200 troop horses'.

Transport meant ships; Mr Herries, the Commissary-General, was writing from the War Office to the Commissioners of Transport. A hundred wagon drivers had already embarked at Deptford; again would they 'be pleased to appoint a vessel' for 150 more on Tuesday.

To keep Wellington's force moving and supplied occupied eight separate departments. The Office of Commander-in-Chief in Horse Guards, Whitehall, prescribed tactics, drill, discipline, and appointed officers – foisting some blunderers on Wellington in deference to seniority. The army was fed by the Commissary-General, shot or flogged by order of the Advocate General, patched up and discharged by a Medical Board, its artillery and engineers controlled separately by the Board of Ordnance, and moved by the Commissioners of Transport. Where it was actually sent depended on the War Department at Downing Street, and its administration, such as it was, on the War Office at Carlton House. Miraculously, the system almost worked.

London docks

7

CAVALRY OUTPOSTS

At Quatre Bras, the first infantry were already off. Sgt Robertson, rejoining his 92nd Highlanders with a bandaged head wound, noticed that 'the cavalry by this time were coming up in great strength'. General 'Daddy' Hill, popular commander of II Corps, was spotted and given 'three hearty cheers'. Wellington joined him; men heard Hill singing their praises; Wellington agreed 'he knew what we could do, and that bye and bye he would give us something to keep our hands in use'. As more cavalry arrived, more and more infantry took the road; a constant show of strength along the ridge helped disguise from the French all signs of retreat. Arrangements were working smoothly; under a hot sun Wellington 'then lay himself down on the ground, covered his head with one of the newspapers he had been reading, and appeared to fall asleep', near General Vivian, commander of 6th Cavalry Brigade, of Hussars. In front of the skirmish line the French were now very quiet. British outposts could see neither them nor their own support troops behind.

Cavalry were to screen the last stages of withdrawal. Surgeon Haddy James, with 1st Life Guards, noticed some clouds appearing; midday had become sultry. 'Some of our men discovered some porter in a nearby farm house ...' Officers were lying in the shade of their cloaks propped 'upon sticks'. Orders to mount, ready for action and to empty haynets turned out a false alarm, and one captain shared a bit of tongue from his valise; 'we drank the wine out of Cox's little leather bucket' – hot, but delicious. By now red lines of marching infantry could be seen along the Genappe road; no longer rumours of an 'advance to Paris'.

To another surgeon, John Smith, with 12th Light Dragoons, strangeness and waiting made the day seem extraordinarily long; thinking it near evening he was astonished to find his watch read 'not yet 12 o'clock'.

Other roads north were full of troops. No more movement east from Nivelles; all regiments from there being diverted direct to Mont St Jean. One lad straight from England, William Leeke, wore the brand new uniform of Ensign in the crack 52nd Light Infantry in Adam's Brigade. On Friday, without warning, a staff officer had ridden up to the captain taking parade. 'Your company, Sir, is to be a mile on the Ath road in twenty minutes from this time.' With bugles calling assembly and men running, the whole regiment formed in column, and from that moment made an almost non-stop march: Ath, then Enghien, a two-hour halt for beef, several miles towards Hal, redirected towards Mons, reaching Braine le Comte at midnight in heavy rain. Two and a half hours' rest, then on again through the small hours to reach Nivelles at 7 a.m. This morning in an orchard, then marching again at noon. All but two of the sixty officers of the 52nd were mounted, but loaded, tramping men were fainting under the pace. By nightfall, they would have carried their muskets and packs fifty miles in thirty-five hours.

Nivelles echoed to troops all last night and all this morning. Mitchell's Brigade, following Adam's, was halted to let Belgian cavalry through – 'fine looking fellows, and much resembled our Blues,' thought Sgt William Wheeler. They were in such haste that for a moment the British thought they were charging, but it transpired they had had enough; they were running away.

Wheeler's section was in luck, pocketing a dropped purse of silver. In the same brigade George Keppel's regiment, 3/14th, had left tear-stained faces when they marched from Acren playing 'The girl we left behind us', but that was thirty miles ago. Fifes were silent now, no songs or jokes among the tired columns.

At Quatre Bras, Wellington could scarcely believe Napoleon was allowing a whole army to withdraw without some reaction. He rode towards the front with Vivian, frequently pausing to use his glass, and 'expressing his astonishment at the perfect quiet of the enemy'. He even wondered if they might be retiring too.

All infantry except forward skirmish lines had left by 1 p.m. Heavy cavalry, Ponsonby's and Somerset's Brigades, were ready to take the centre road, Grant's and Vivian's Hussars ranged right and left as a forward screen, Vandeleur's Light Dragoons behind in a second line.

Mercer was back near the crossroads, 'left with my troop, quite alone, on the brow of the position'. As horse artillery, he had been assigned to Somerset's Brigade, but never found them. All spare ammunition wagons had gone, leaving only gun limbers with fifty rounds each; he felt dangerously exposed, forgotten. The Earl of Uxbridge, commanding all cavalry, and an aide rode up, dismounted and sat watching the French position through glasses. The aide detected smoke. 'It will not be long ... they always dine before they move,' he warned. Lt William Hay, in 12th Light Dragoons, noticed a change in the distance: 'clouds of dust began to spread over the trees.' Uxbridge saw it too and galloped away, shouting 'By the Lord they are Prussians!' Downhill Vivian had his telescope up: on the Namur road, distant about three miles, he detected 'something glittering in the sun ...' Wellington thought they were bayonets; Vivian decided the pin-points were cuirassiers. Hay could see them now, 'as if by magic, debouched from the dark green foliage ... the gorgeous uniforms of the French cavalry ...'

Wellington and Uxbridge rode down closer, in front of 10th Hussars. Capt. Taylor heard 'the Duke say, "Well, I suppose we shall fight them here."' Uxbridge objected: for cavalry fighting cavalry the ground was too broken behind. Wellington, 'stretching himself and yawning', remarked coolly, 'Then I suppose we must retreat.'

French were forming fast. As last British infantry pickets retired uphill they could see them too. George Simmons's Riflemen were amazed; in Spain they had never witnessed massed cavalry ranged 'like a field day'. Simmons laughed: 'Look at them, my lads, tomorrow if it please God we will have a regular turn up with them . . .'

Mercer was worried by the sheer size of French concentration; his guns were the only ones in sight. He pulled his troop back to 2nd cavalry line, where Uxbridge ordered him to prepare for action: 'Let them get well up before you fire.' He warned Mercer to be ready for instant limbering up and a last-minute getaway.

As guns were unhooked and trained and loaded, Mercer had time to notice 'large isolated masses of thunder cloud . . . their lower edges hard and strongly defined . . . while the distant hill . . . still lay bathed in brilliant sunshine.'

A single figure sat silhouetted – almost certainly Napoleon himself.

The time was 2 p.m.

8

*G*ALLOP THROUGH THE RAIN

The long wait was almost over. A moaning wind was piling up storm clouds to blot out the sky; gleaming against an inky darkness, lances and pennants of French cavalry were ranged in massed lines, squadron by squadron. With a ripple of harness they moved forward. Capt. Taylor of 10th Hussars saw Vivian's outposts driven in by skirmish fire and saw the flashes of a Royal Horse Artillery battery 'knocking men and horses off the road', then bugles sounded 'threes about' and the regiment was in retreat. The French brought up guns and caught some British in the hollow of a cornfield, but otherwise kept to a westward advance along the Nivelles road.

Vandeleur's Light Dragoons in the second line had already moved. One officer with the 16th, Capt. Tomkinson, saw the French coming out 'column after column, and in greater force than I ever recollect seeing together at one point'. Hay's squadron was the first ordered to wheel away. Before they could, the heavens ripped open, dropping 'torrents of rain ... with such violence in our teeth that ... our horses with spurs stuck in their flanks would not keep their heads to the storm.' Crowded in narrow lanes, hooves slipping, with cries from the rear of 'faster, faster in front', Hay's regiment plunged back towards the river Dyle. Behind Vandeleur's, Vivian's Brigade too was making for a pre-arranged route which forded the river east of Genappe.

Mercer's battery with 7th Hussars and 23rd Light Dragoons was guarding the main centre road. As oncoming squadrons formed on the hill opposite, Uxbridge himself shouted 'Fire!' Sheets of rain driving slantwise almost blinded the gun teams, thunder drowned their explosions, and answering flashes from French artillery paled to pin-points in the glare of lightning. Fiery trails from a British rocket battery ploughed through the corn, but the French were advancing fast; Mercer had barely time for one round per gun before ordering 'rear limber-up'; and gun trails hooked to limbers, drivers lashing their horses to a gallop, they were racing for the road.

Heavy cavalry, mounted in a rear defence line behind the crossroads, got the orders to retire and began leapfrogging back through German cavalry, amid 'rye as tall as ourselves on horseback', wrote Surgeon James. Muddy and alarmed, he was heartened at passing Wellington with his staff, looking 'very cheerful and smiling'. His unit, 1st Life Guards, formed up in a new position across a hill behind Genappe.

With Uxbridge riding beside him, Mercer gained Quatre Bras hamlet just as rearguard infantry pulled out. Simmons took 'a last look at the pot of soup' someone had started, 'groaned in spirit', then, blanket across his shoulders, set off under the downpour. Uxbridge urged the guns faster; taking a wrong turning they found it barred by the French. 'By God, we are all prisoners!' Uxbridge leaped a wall, leaving Mercer's men to unlimber again and haul the trails of their guns around by hand before they could retreat. Amazingly, the French seemed paralysed. Mercer passed the last British cavalry on the south bank of the Dyle, and with shouts and even taunting laughter of the French now at his back splashed over Genappe bridge and up its cobbled street. The centre gutter was like a river, but as he rode out of the deserted town he could see main lines of Life Guards and the Horse Guards or Blues stretching across the road ahead.

The south side of the bridge was covered by a rearguard squadron of 7th Hussars. Its officer, Lt O'Grady, had been reminded by General Dornberg, Brigade Commander of Light Dragoons, that it was vital 'to face the enemy boldly' to give skirmishers time to struggle in from the heavy fields each side. By continually half-advancing and threatening, O'Grady kept the French at bay until last skirmishers were across, then one by one his men filed away and 'passed through the town at a gallop'. Dornberg greeted him with grim surprise: 'Then Buonaparte is not with them; if he were, not a man of you would have escaped.'

Despite much shouting and noise it was nearly twenty minutes before the head of a French column emerged from the far side. Some isolated stragglers had already blundered into British lines, quite drunk. As the French appeared in force, 7th were ordered to charge. Swords clashed with lances, horses slithered and fell in the walled bottleneck jammed with cavalry until the British, their rear caught in gunfire, were forced to retreat, leaving the road 'strewn with men'. One of their officers, Capt. Verner, thought 'they might just as well have charged a house!'

The French were advancing uphill by now. 23rd Light Dragoons, seeing the 7th streaming back, hesitated; Uxbridge angrily ordered them aside: 'The Life Guards shall have this honour.' Heavier men on big horses thundered down and savagely toppled the lancers bodily back into the town. The French brought up more guns; Mercer was ordered through a morass to bring his teams somehow into action. Getting the range quickly, he opened counter-battery fire. Surgeon James, left in a hollow behind cavalry lines, found himself amidst heavy shelling coming over the hill. He was driven up to the crest, 'but on the top ... a staff officer ... recommended me in no uncertain terms to get out of the battle at once, as I might be taken or piked ... in any case I was of no service up there.' Unarmed, he recognized good advice and was going back when he was caught up by the Life Guards, retreating now, hardly a patch of red showing through a solid coating of mud, even faces 'hardly distinguishable'. Without his instruments, he could do nothing for the wounded lying across their saddles.

Through blinding rain squalls interminable columns of British infantry were marching steadily north. Off minor roads to the east, Halkett's Brigade, knee deep in mire, had halted as rearguard to let Kempt's through. Furthest ahead on central

Brussels road was Pack's Brigade. Tiredness and overcrowding slowed movement to a crawl. The 92nd was overtaken by a wagon carrying the body of the young and popular Duke of Brunswick, killed yesterday, 'the corpse ... with the fatal wound, in the breast, exposed to public view.' Lt Hope saw the soldiers escorting it point to the body, swearing revenge.

Drawing well ahead of the cavalry, all V Division halted for one hour in fields, to allow a drum-head court martial to sentence some men for wasting ammunition. No one standing before the tight-lipped disciplinarian Picton could have guessed that his soiled civilian coat (his uniform had been left behind in the rush from Brussels) hid a bandaged wound from yesterday which gave him constant pain but which he kept secret from all but his servant.

On again soon after 4 p.m., the division ploughed through roads almost obliterated. Eastern route even worse. Somewhere in the murk Ensign Macready, standing in infantry line with the 2/30th was passed by Hussars caked 'from spur to plume'. 'Rained so violently ... prevented General Vivian consulting the map,' reported Lt Duperier, adjutant of 18th. Splashing lost through deserted hamlets they at last found one peasant as guide, 'placed behind Trumpeter Verity ... on his horse'.

The appalling weather actually helped the Allies; with no accurate knowledge of what lay in front the French could only feel their way. Cavalry was suddenly useless; fast reconnaissance impossible across fields turned quagmires. Napoleon's one anxiety was that Wellington might escape before he could be brought to battle. Soon after his capture in the fiasco at Genappe, Capt. Elphinstone of the 7th Hussars was brought wounded before the Emperor for questioning. Did Wellington intend to retreat all the way to Brussels? Elphinstone 'could not tell'. Staff officers insisted on a reply. Elphinstone was adamant: 'I am not in his Grace's secrets.' His pocket spilled an English newspaper as he was helped away. A French officer spotted it. 'Is that the *Morning Post* or the *Chronicle*?' he asked, and then let slip that he had been in London only three days before – clearly as a spy.

Mercer's battery was keeping pace with cavalry rearguard, retreating step by step, firing from positions hastily formed on each hill by turn. With ammunition almost gone and no supply wagons near, at one point he left his guns and joined a rocket team, hoping they would disguise the slow rate of fire from his battery. Capt. Whinyates, R.H.A., was proud of his new Congreve rockets; the first one, trailing its twenty-foot pole behind, flared straight down the road to explode under an enemy gun and caused wild confusion, but the rest lived up to Wellington's distrust of the things. Rising straight up, sometimes looping backwards to threaten the British, zig-zagging crazily, they flew anywhere except where aimed. French gunners soon returned to their pieces, and Lancers pressed forward as much as they could short of actually charging. Retreating again, Mercer's teams ran into rear of Brunswick infantry, and before he could explain panicked them into headlong flight across the fields: 'away went arms and knapsacks in all directions ...'

By 6 p.m. leading British infantry were climbing the low crest before Mont St Jean, where waiting staff officers led them to allotted areas. 92nd had time to notice the whitewashed buildings of a farm which split their line; then a final plod uphill to a blessed halt behind a hedge which straggled beside a narrow cross road. Other regiments continued a defence line right and left.

All afternoon further brigades had been converging towards the main Brussels road from Nivelles. Adam's was in the lead, setting off at 4.30 p.m. after a two-hour halt, but yesterday's heat and today's storm had taken their toll. 'Each side of the road was now *lined* with soldiers of different regiments, and with some women and drummer-boys, who had fallen out from fatigue,' noted Ensign Leeke, with 52nd. The sky was beginning to clear at last. In the rain-washed air Leeke, on horseback, caught occasional glimpses of the Brussels highway only a mile and a half to his right. French cavalry could be recognized; the regiment halted 'still in open column of companies, and loaded'. On the march again, Leeke spotted two French staff officers making notes, only a few hundred yards away, before they rode off.

Towards 7 p.m., allied cavalry and artillery were coming up through Picton's defence screen. Kempt's and Pack's Brigades were mostly in; 95th Rifles placed in 2nd line. The 92nd Highlanders had already cleaned their muskets and put them in order, when Sgt Robertson walked to the far edge of the road bordering their position, where a second hedge hid the view. The valley below displayed a sight to catch the breath of even a veteran. Under an angry sky, the van of Napoleon's army was descending an opposing ridge only two miles away, swelling and spreading outwards. 'Such numerous columns I had never looked on before, nor do I believe any man in the British Army had ever seen such a host.' Robertson worried at the thinness of his line; but at least 'our artillery and a rocket-brigade had now arrived, all the cavalry ... and a great number of foreign infantry ...'

French light cavalry was still pressing the rearguard. Mercer's battery was the last artillery to come in, retreating one more lap through the valley to 'a capital position on the top of an old gravel pit'. A high hedge hid all view of Picton's division behind. Mercer waited for a large body of French lancers to come within extreme range before letting loose at 1,200 yards. Before the echo of his first gun died away, 'to my astonishment, a heavy cannonade' opened up behind him; 'the truth now flashed on me, we had rejoined the army.' More French batteries came into action; artillery fire swelled on both sides until it seemed the start of battle.

Leeke's 52nd was taking a right-hand fork towards a country
house when the crest ahead burst into flame; they could see
fierce skirmishing and heavy smoke before new orders sent
them back on the main road to Mont St Jean. Across a hill-top
the men cheered some Light Dragoons riding past, straight out
of action.

As Mercer's men were swabbing out their gun barrels a
civilian in a 'drab greatcoat and a rusty round hat' walked down
from the hill and began asking questions. Mercer cut him short;
and, ignored and unrecognized, General Picton returned to his
lines. Fighting was dying down now; it seemed clear the French,
knowing now that Wellington's army was in force, were preparing to halt. An old soldier reassured young Leeke as they passed
over the crest: 'there will be no battle tonight ... all the Duke
of Wellington's great battles have been fought on a Sunday.'
They were directed on, through hedges, down reverse slopes
behind the main line, to a ploughed field on the west flank.
Behind Adam's, Mitchell's Brigade was last infantry to arrive.
Col. Tidy of 3/14th knew the country; on a rise of ground he
pointed out a distant spire, announcing, 'That is Waterloo.' His
men filed past a welcome tub of gin before marching still further
to their place in rear reserve, near Merbe Braine.
   Rain had set in again, but Sgt Wheeler's cronies in next
regiment, 51st, had their own cure. 'One man in the village was
selling brandy and hollands, the money picked up a few hours
before procured us plenty of both, and some bread and cheese
... we were ... "wet and comfortable".'

By the cluster of cottages forming Mont St Jean, Wellington
was still in the saddle after nearly nine hours' riding. Reports
from divisional and brigade H.Q.s added up to remove his
worst worry: a potentially disastrous retreat in the face of an
active enemy had succeeded brilliantly, with almost no loss.
Only Lambert's Brigade, still to march up from Brussels, was
not now in approximate position on the ridge. Since the precise
strength of French in front was anybody's guess, it was still
possible that Napoleon's main thrust would be a wide sweep to
try to outflank Wellington's right; to counter this, 15,000

British, Hanoverian and Dutch troops had been kept detached around Tubize to watch roads and open country to the west. As for the left, the Prussians should have reached Wavre, only nine miles away. Wellington knew Blücher's reputation as a fighter; unless Napoleon split his army for a double attack, a link tomorrow between the Allies seemed certain.

Among orders streaming in and out from his advanced H.Q., a message arrived at 8 p.m. from Waterloo, two miles to the rear. At the main inn, supper was ready and waiting.

9

ℒONDON INTERLUDE

In London, the Commander-in-Chief of all British land forces had well and truly started his. The Duke of York was one of five Dukes (the others being Clarence, Kent, Sussex, Devonshire), five Lords (Westmoreland, Shaftesbury, Buckingham, Bathurst, Liverpool), the Chancellor of the Exchequer, the Attorney General and other big-wigs invited to a 'magnificent dinner' at the Mansion House by Mr Birch, the Lord Mayor. Turtle soup in silver, powdered footmen, toasts in Madeira, and not the slightest suspicion of events across the Channel to spoil a single appetite.

Private dinner parties were ending – most people sat down at six. Walnuts and fruit were piled beside bowls of rose water for wiping fingers, while women withdrew to leave to men the serious business of sporting gossip, more port and the aroma of cigars.

The evening was warm: 60 degrees recorded at 11 p.m.; and lighted candelabra were already glowing through the open

Mansion House

View of Park Lane

windows of elegant houses in Grosvenor and Berkeley Squares. With rooms stripped of spare furniture and footmen scrubbed and gloved, society hostesses were beginning final preparations for the evening's 'routs', when the first crunch of carriage wheels at 10 p.m. would signal a flood of guests.

Flares were smoking in Tottenham Court Road and Islington and Shoreditch for Saturday's street markets. Offal, tripe, trotters and cheap vegetables would be on sale until well past midnight – long after theatres would have closed, even after the bemused crowds would have stumbled from the marathon show at Astley's Amphitheatre by Westminster Bridge. Twenty-one scenes of 'Harlequin on Horseback', a comic play 'King Henry VIII and the cobbler', a ballet, and 'a real Fox

Lobby of Drury Lane Theatre

Aquatic Theatre at Sadler's Wells

Chace' were advertised there, while guns were blazing – without shot – at a spectacular 'Battle of the Nile' fought 'on real water' at Sadler's Wells. Dog fights at Westminster Pit, sparring gloves for hire in sawdust pubs, beggars, fiddlers, street showmen:

Winchester Street, London Wall

among all the varied scenes of the capital one of the most
famous was missing. The shining mails, armed guard beside
each driver, had left a full hour before. Harness gleaming, every
night they swung off their stands precisely at 7.30 for all parts
of the kingdom. Well clear of town now, the Dover Mail, with
letters – franked at the cheap rate of 1d. for soldiers – for
Wellington's army in its trunk, had already breasted Shooter's
Hill, and under a fine sky was running down to Dartford.

Ahead, beyond the coastline, the Channel sea was dark under
a freshening wind; the storm belt over France was moving
slowly north. Troopships in *Sharpshooter* convoy had reached
to within three miles of Ostend, but having missed the flood tide
to carry them into harbour were hove to. Ships rolled uneasily,
all of them dangerously overloaded, some leaking. Ensign
Bakewell's vessel, *Dawson*, had already 'been near aground'.

$\mathcal{B}$IVOUACS, FIRES, FOOD

To dying artillery fire, Wellington and Delancey were riding along the ridge of the position by a cross road leading west. The sky ahead was streaked with the after-glow of sunset; already first dusk softened the outlines of dripping hedges in a valley to the left. There the immensely strong buildings of a mansion and its farm, set in extensive walled grounds, formed the largest man-made feature between Wellington and Napoleon. Scattered musketry echoed from woods and orchard occupied by French skirmishers.

The whole estate, screened by trees and ideal as a protected concentration area from which to cover an attack, was far too close to be left in enemy hands; and four light companies of Guards were ordered down from the ridge to take it.

Private Matthew Clay's company was sheltering from the rain, each four men under two blankets pegged over up-ended rifles as makeshift tent poles, when they got the order to move. Clay was left to pack up, strap his soaked blanket and follow as best he could. Doubling downhill past British batteries, he slipped up to his neck in a flooded ditch, barely managed to haul himself out, and dripping wet joined his mates lining an orchard hedge. With the French driven back into the woods in front, they lay shivering, muskets in hand, on constant alert.

From west to east, forward slopes of the position were guarded by pickets. Ensign Short, with Coldstream Guards, was 'under arms the whole night expecting an attack'. Rain now a steady downpour. On the left flank, where the ridge levelled off into marshy ground, dismounted cavalry watched for Prussians as well as French, with units like Hay's 12th Light Dragoons 'knee deep' in water.

Behind the picket lines the main army prepared to bivouac as best it could. During the years in the Peninsula officers of the old Light Division had perfected a technique: with a convenient tree at their backs, they barricaded themselves on each side with saddles, canteens and portmanteaux, and built a blazing fire in front to keep out the cold. But this was no stony hillside in Spain, and two days' forced marching and retreat had disorganized all supplies except ammunition. The 95th was shaking down in a sodden trampled cornfield in the 2nd line. With his horse tethered to a bayonet pinning a bundle of fodder, Lt Kincaid, the regiment's adjutant, laid another bundle alongside for himself. Men were too exhausted to be particular: another officer of the 95th, Capt. Leach, already drenched, prepared to lie in ground as wet as 'a snipe marsh'.

Amid all the rain, almost no fresh water. Squelching through mud to their knees, some men from the 92nd followed Hope to Waterloo, in vain. 'Draw-wells ... in abundance, but not a single rope.' Wells too deep even for '23 canteen straps, buckled together', and the party returned to face the torments of cold, hunger, and now thirst.

A prime need was fuel. Troopers from 12th Light Dragoons were among the first with axe and bill-hook in Mont St Jean: doors, window shutters, carts, ploughs, tables were soon chopped and blazing. Chairs to sit on were sold for £2 by the men. Some officers found shelter of sorts; 100 yards from the village Dalrymple's 15th Hussars crawled under 'some little straw huts' left by Belgian haymakers, but they kept out 'neither wind nor rain'.

As last daylight faded, the great belt of forest to the rear became one black mass. Wheatley, with his party from the King's German Legion, had halted there on his way from Genappe, and, determined now to return tomorrow to his unit, broke open a barn. Further back along the road, Lambert's Brigade 'crept into any hole we could find, cowsheds, cart-houses . . .' wrote Sgt William Lawrence of 40th. 'All night was one continual clamour, for thousands of camp followers were on their retreat to Brussels.' Southwards, but still well in rear of main position, Mercer had led his battery over the ridge to bivouac in the enticing green of a roadside orchard belonging to Mont St Jean farm. The 'smiling turf' turned out to be a swamp, but it was too late to move the guns. One abandoned sack of grain fed his horses; for himself and his men, 'absolutely nothing!' Nearby farm buildings were filled with cavalry; his hungry gunners crawled under the carriages and limbers while officers bravely erected a small tent amid the water.

It was almost dark when at 9.30 p.m. Wellington turned his sweating horse Copenhagen into the yard of Waterloo's main inn. Not the fastest or most handsome of horses, Wellington said later, 'but for bottom and endurance I never saw his fellow'. In case he should need him again in the night, he ordered his groom 'to give him no hay, but after a few go-downs of chilled water, as much corn and beans as he had a mind for'. Wellington then ate a light meal himself before resuming work in his private room.

The main question concerned Blücher. So far there had been no answer to Wellington's promise this morning to stand and fight. A second appeal was drafted: Wellington's army was now in position but vitally needed support of 'at least one corps' in tomorrow's expected battle. Could Blücher march, with what strength, and how soon?

As an aide rode off along the miry lanes to Wavre, British, Dutch, German, Belgian troops of the army were settling in. More fires were spluttering and smoking; Capt. Tomkinson heard one of his officers calling to a trooper of 16th Light Dragoons staggering 'out of the village of Waterloo with a clock on his back'. The trooper shouted to come and see how he would 'make the beggar tick', and set the grandfather case over some sticks as a chimney.

In last glimmer of light, A.D.C.s were leading units to final areas. Leeke's 52nd looked strangely like figures in a Japanese print: falling in at 10 p.m. to march nearer the crest each man humped not only musket, blanket and pack but on his head a sodden bundle of thatch, torn from cottage roofs, before lying down again in new lines. Robertson's 92nd found 'a field of green clover'; cut and stiffened with hedgerow branches, it made a rough matting over the clay.

Nearly everyone hungry. Gibney, junior surgeon with Dalrymple's Hussars, at least had had a bit of tongue earlier in the day, and with a thimbleful of brandy in his flask realized he was luckier than most. Others had spirits: Black of the 3/1st Guards wrote, 'without fire with our swords in our hand expecting the French would advance in the night ... it was dreadful beyond description the way I and all of us did we had double allowance of gin and we poured it down our throats while we lay on our backs till we dropped off asleep ...'

Whole central area was by now stripped of food, but Taylor, with 10th Hussars on far east flank, found some of the officers

in a cottage 'picking and broiling fowls'. Close to the main road, 1/95th had somehow laid hands on first supplies from Brussels: Simmons was called to a weaver's shop and presented with 'a plump bird of some sort', with wine, porter and cigars from Col. Barnard's private stock. 'Stop, Sir, you may have four.' Tongues were wagging. Huge Col. Elley, bloodstained sword on display, was boasting of his charge with the Horse Guards; he personally had never 'made better practice … they really went down before me like children'. Simmons refused to stay, however, preferring to rough it with his men. 'George, you are a strange fellow,' observed Barnard as he left.

Back in the lines, snug under one blanket plastered with clay as water-proofing, on top of a second, with knapsacks for pillows, Simmons and a friend were soon lulled to sleep by the drumming of the rain. In the same regiment lanky Johnny Kincaid, stretched beside his horse, had learned in past campaigns to sleep through any noise except the bugle; 'never opened my eyes again until daylight.'

Some fifteen miles south-east, two French army corps were filing into flooded fields, also trying to bivouac. Marshal Grouchy had sent off the van of Napoleon's right wing early in the afternoon, but terrible roads slowed his advance to only nine miles by nightfall. At 9 p.m. his rearguard was still trailing in to Gembloux when, with troops famished and dropping, he ordered a halt.

Worried though he was, Grouchy nevertheless wrote Napoleon late at night that the pursuit was going well: one Prussian column sighted by his cavalry at Tourinnes did indeed appear to be trying to join Wellington, but the bulk of Blücher's army, he wrote, was safely heading due east for Liège and the German frontier. What Grouchy didn't know was that the Prussians reported by peasants eastwards at Perwez were in fact Blücher's rearmost army corps marching up towards Wavre, not the other way.

Nearer, at Genappe on the Quatre Bras road, another French general picked up some disturbing gossip. Foy was dining with Prince Jerome, Napoleon's brother, in the *Roi d'Espagne* inn. A waiter whispered that he had overheard an English officer, in the same room earlier in the day, say that 'the English army would await the French at the entrance to the Forest of Soignes', where the Prussians would join it. The first part was hardly news, but a possible Prussian link-up was. Jerome made a note to tell the Emperor in the morning.

At 11 p.m. a muddy dispatch rider reached Wavre and delivered Wellington's letter. The earlier message had gone astray. Blücher was roused, and joined by Gneisenau, Chief of Staff. Three Prussian army corps were bivouacked in the surrounding area; the fourth, under General Bülow, was now only four miles east, but a march across the line of enemy advance, should Napoleon drive north again against the Prussians, could be disastrous. Gneisenau had already experienced one near-disaster. While the argument continued, the English liaison officer, Col. Hardinge, nursing the stump of an arm lost at Ligny, waited anxiously outside.

In Waterloo, senior officers were thankfully turning in to their quarters. Col. Frazer added a footnote to his letter home: 'June 17, 11 p.m. Just arrived from the front, tired, jaded, dirty, and going to bed ... tomorrow I start before daybreak. – Adieu.'

The white houses had names chalked on nearly every door; Wellington's had a late caller. Before he finally retired, the Earl of Uxbridge tried to allay one nagging fear. Should Wellington be killed he, Uxbridge, would succeed to command of the army

– but so far without any plans to go on. Although two generals had each referred him to the Duke, Uxbridge spoke nervously. An elopement with Wellington's brother's wife, his present appointment from London against Wellington's direct wishes, his own flamboyant personality, hardly made him his commander's best friend.

The Duke cut him short.

'Who will attack the first tomorrow, I or Bonaparte?'

'Bonaparte.'

'Well, Bonaparte has not given me any idea of his projects; and as my plans will depend upon his, how can you expect me to tell you what mine are?'

But he softened his words '... whatever happens, you and I will do our duty.'

As midnight struck, both Allied and French armies were marked by watchfires, stretching four miles and more; 'one of the most beautiful sights I ever saw,' thought one soldier, Pte Lewis, of the 2/95th. Out in the valley, Napoleon himself was watching through the teeming rain, making a last tour of his position. The glowing ridge left him no possible doubt; Wellington's despised, motley army was waiting in force; tomorrow by all odds it would be swept into oblivion. Grimly satisfied, the Emperor returned to his H.Q. at Le Caillou.

Wellington, orders and tasks finished, also lay down and was almost instantly asleep. Outside, the rattle and splash of horse-drawn wagons moving up to the front continued all night.

At Wavre, midnight brought a message to the anxious
Hardinge to report to Blücher. The indomitable old man had
won. 'Gneisenau has given in. We're going to join the Duke,'
he cried jubilantly. Actually the cautious Gneisenau had made
conditions: leading corps was to be the one furthest away; and
first march would be only to Chapelle St Lambert, some miles
short of Mont St Jean. But Hardinge was not to know all this;
he took the letter thankfully, and within minutes a British rider
was on his way to Waterloo.

On one sector at Mont St Jean, bugles and shouts called the
42nd and 92nd of Pack's infantry stiffly to their feet for a whole
hour's shivering stand-to; but threatened attack turned out to
have been only Belgian cavalry shifting position, and replying
to British sentries in French.

Another area with no rest was Hougoumont. Light companies of Coldstream Guards were working there in shifts from
sentry duty, under a huge Highlander, Lt-Col. Macdonell.
With greasy, slipping tools they were driving loopholes through
garden walls, building earth banks and wooden firing platforms
behind, blocking all gates except the main entrance facing
north, and prising up floorboards over the south gateway so
riflemen could fire down between the joists on any attackers
below.

Night an endless purgatory. '... Lay in a bean-field ... almost drowned in water,' wrote William Pritchard of the Guards. Hay was so exhausted he collapsed on a ridge of mud. Sgt Tom Morris and others in Halkett's Brigade, half-buried in a sloping cornfield, bundled stalks into mats for their knapsacks and perched on top, blankets over their heads. For hours they could clearly hear the French rustling and moving in the valley. At 1 a.m., the 92nd was relieved from stand-to; frozen stiff, they tried to forget their misery by sitting in pairs, with their backs to the storm, swapping tales or humming Highland songs. And everywhere long lines of restless horses glistened in the darkness. In the bogs southwards, those of French lancers and cuirassiers even worse off, many carrying the weight of riders dozing all night in the saddle.

Wellington had had just two hours' rest when he was awakened at 2 a.m. to receive Blücher's letter. As he broke the seal and read the long-awaited words he felt a great load roll from his mind.

'Bülow's Corps will set off marching tomorrow at daybreak ... immediately followed by the Corps of Pirch. The 1st and 3rd Corps will also hold themselves in readiness ...'

Although it would clearly take several hours to move two complete army corps in the present state of roads, they should be in action before the climax of any coming battle. With complete faith in the old warrior's word, he knew he would not now be fighting alone.

Others were rising too. At Mont St Jean farm a bedraggled Mercer was finally driven from a tent which leaked like a sieve and he gave up all further thoughts of sleep. To his 'infinite joy' he discovered some men smoking pipes around two fires. His second captain joined him, and with borrowed sticks they soon had their own 'cheerful blaze' under a hedge. With Capt. Newland's despised umbrella set over them against a bank, and cigars lit, they at last 'became – comfortable'. Towards the ridge, young Keppel was woken from a 'mountain torrent' and taken to a small cottage, where fragments of chairs, tables, window-frames, were burning in the fire-place. Three older men sitting in underclothes, drying out, made room for him without speaking. It was only later that the boy saw that one uniform over a chair back carried colonel's epaulettes; the owner was Sir John Colborne, commanding officer of the famous 52nd.

By 3 a.m., Wellington was dressed and writing letters of reassurance to Brussels. One was to the British Ambassador: 'Pray keep the English quiet if you can. Let them all prepare to move, but neither be in a hurry or a fright, as all will yet turn out well.'

Down the street, Frazer was also up and writing in his own billet. 'Waterloo, June 18, 3 a.m. Quite refreshed after a comfortable night's rest ... We retired to a position previously selected, and we shall now make a stand ...'

Sunday 18 June 1815

11

*D*AWN

Darkness was perhaps a fraction lighter; sunrise less than an hour away. The half-silence was suddenly broken by a bugle, then others, then hoarse shouts and commands. Along more than two miles of hillside all front line units dragged themselves from sodden blankets, groped for muskets, and bending against the rain formed double lines facing south. On active service, 'stand-to', to guard against surprise dawn attack, ran from one hour before sunrise to about one hour after – officially until 'a grey horse can be seen a mile off'. Waiting silent, unmoving, on an empty stomach made this the worst time of any day.

The 92nd could hardly hold their weapons. Sgt Robertson 'never felt colder in my life; every one of us was shaking like an aspen leaf'. Higher up the ridge. Halkett's Brigade even more exposed: Macready's regiment 'almost petrified ... many could not stand ...' One Irish officer, legs useless, fell in the mud again and again, becoming frantic from 'the dread that he should not be able to do his duty'.

But the minutes slowly passed, and as the sky lightened the rain lessened too. A weak sunrise at 3.50 was enough to cheer most spirits. The rolling outlines of the French position became visible, with no apparent sign of attack. As one by one units fell out, much work had to be tackled before food or rest. Urgent priorities were horses for cavalry, and muskets for infantry.

Capt. Grove's journal: 'After the desperate weather ... neither men nor horses looked worth a shilling a piece.' His own so 'knocked up ... I sent him to Brussels ... I was obliged to ride a trooper.' Most cavalrymen had ditched their hay fodder bundles. Lt Elliot in 2nd Life Guards gathered some unripe wheat straw to rub his horse down, 'as I thought it would refresh him'.

The main weapon of all infantrymen, indeed of battle itself, was the musket – or in some special units the new grooved rifle. They were wet, muddy, but still loaded. Cleaning meant unloading, and the quickest way to clear a rammed ball and cartridge was to fire them off: the 'infernal clatter' of musketry throughout the lines made Mercer, nearly a mile to the rear, wonder if an attack had started. For a good hour men were wiping and oiling, making ready for inspection. Cartridges were counted, barrels and vent holes and powder pans cleared, flints tested for spark and reset in cocking handles. Clay, with the Guards in an orchard ditch, found his wooden stock so swollen from water and rain it was jamming the lock spring.

After officers had inspected arms, fuel, water and food parties set off to scour the countryside. Wheeler's 51st had taken new ground, where nearby cottages were soon ripped apart to make 'some good fires'. Not far away, Leeke wandered off to a blaze made by 71st Highlanders. Despite his bed of straw he had slept little; horses broken loose from some cavalry pickets had galloped to and fro all night, and when he did doze off it was to a nightmare of close battle. He now set a spare plank in the mud, and stretching himself before the fire slept a full three hours. By the crossroads, Kincaid awoke to disaster – an adjutant without a horse. To find his missing charger 'among ten thousand others' seemed hopeless, but after an hour's nerve-racking search he tracked him down to an artillery battery.

Soon after 4 a.m., Wellington rode out from headquarters at the head of some forty horsemen: his Military Secretary, Col. Fitzroy Somerset; eight personal A.D.C.s; General Muffling, the Prince of Orange, Uxbridge, the Adjutant General, Deputy Quartermaster General Delancey, Chiefs of Artillery and Engineers – all with their separate staffs – and foreign generals and visitors, including the Spanish General Alava – the only man present today who had fought at Trafalgar, ten years ago, against Nelson. On their way to the front they overtook one young Guards officer, Ensign Gronow, returning from guarding prisoners in Waterloo. Splashed and muddy in the rutted roadside, he thought the jingling cavalcade looked 'as gay and unconcerned as if they were riding to meet the hounds in some quiet English county'.

It was dull and drizzling but full day when Wellington passed Mont St Jean and halted where the sunken cross road which marked his front line crossed the main Genappe highway. Many officers dispersed from here, while Wellington and Muffling with their own staffs began a detailed tour of the position. Muffling, a senior general himself, with considerable battle experience in previous Prussian campaigns against Napoleon, commanded the Duke's confidence and was prepared to give advice. Methodically, beginning with the far right flank, then over the hills behind Hougoumont towards the centre, they began inspecting the position, unit by unit.

Although some fires were burning cheerily, there were no rations yet to cook over them. 2/3 Guards in Hougoumont had only bread crumbs but found a pig; Clay got 'a portion of the head in its rough state', but 'warmed through and blackened with smoke' on the end of his bayonet, the raw mess was too revolting and he put it in his haversack. Some cavalrymen had eaten nothing for two days. Lt Waymouth, 2nd Life Guards, tried horse fodder, 'eating the grain after having rubbed it out from the ear'. 'Nothing but some gin ... from a German woman' kept Capt. Turner, of 13th Light Dragoons, going, and gin too was the only thing that warmed most front line infantry.

Mercer, stationed with his guns, out of touch in the rear, was resigned to another day's retreat on an empty stomach when, rustling through the hedge, a 'godsend' in the guise of 'a poor fellow belonging to some Hanoverian Regiment' appeared, wet through and asking 'permission to ... warm himself by our fire'. After recovering a little he knocked out his pipe and, by way of thanks, produced from his haversack 'a poor half-starved chicken'. The thing soon drew all Mercer's 'gentlemen' around it, watching hungrily. Before it was half-boiled it was 'snatched from the kettle ... pulled to pieces, and speedily devoured'. Mercer got a leg, with 'not one mouthful' on it.

His men were in luck too; battery wagons had found their way up, bringing not only ammunition, but biscuit, beef, oatmeal and rum found abandoned. Rum inside them first, gunners set to work on 'stirabout', but officers decided to bypass porridge and wait for beef stew. Mercer, meanwhile, rode forward to see what was happening.

Passing Mercer's orchard, Wheatley's King's German Legion party came 'up to the Division about five o'clock' and rejoined the 5th Line Battalion to the right of the crossroads. It was still cold and cloudy, but the rain was clearing. As morning wore on, more and more men broke from their tasks for a moment to stare southwards. By 6 a.m., those on the highest part of the ridge could begin to make out changes on the hills opposite. Wheatley realized some large dark masses were slowly moving. Filled with foreboding, with memories of his Eliza in Abingdon, he was fascinated despite himself: 'Where the edge of the ground bound the horizon, shoals of these gloomy bodies glided down, disjointing then contracting ... like melted lava from a Volcano ... While gazing with all my utmost stretch of vision ... little Gerson struck me on the shoulder, saying, "That's a battle, my boy! ... You'd better have stopped with Nötting at Brussels ..."'

Muffling and Wellington were nearing the eastern flank, where the cross road descended lower ground towards the River Lasne and Ohain. Half a mile in front, the clustered hamlets of Papelotte, La Haye and Smohain nestled in a steep valley; beyond them, half a mile further, a parallel road ran also east to Chapelle St Lambert; both roads leading finally to Wavre. Looking at maps, studying the ground with his glass, Muffling pointed out that the French seemed careless here; only isolated cavalry patrols guarded their right beyond the villages. He drew out three alternative routes for a Prussian advance, with a suggested concentration area by the heights of St Lambert. Wellington called, 'I quite agree,' and one of Muffling's aides rode off with the note for Blücher.

If eastern roads were vital for reinforcements, northern ones were even more so for supplies. Infantry still had only marching ammunition, sixty rounds per man in pouches, sixty in haversacks. Wellington had seen for himself the traffic chaos in the

forest of Soignes, and now Col. Scovell, reporting back from supply depots in Brussels, told the Duke that in many places the road was 'completely blocked' by abandoned carts and wagons. Wellington was short and blunt, ordering them cleared, any way Scovell liked, but instantly. 'Take a squadron of Dragoons.'

Riding back uneasily, Scovell found the whole of Lambert's Brigade about to march. He offered a bribe: the wagons for firewood if they cleared the road. The veterans' pride was stung, 'on fire at the idea' of such work when a battle was afoot; but the Brigade A.D.C. Harry Smith reckoned a 'magician's wand' couldn't have cleared a path quicker 'than 3,000 soldiers of the old school'. Beside dripping glades littered with smashed shafts and wheels they formed again in column; this time Smith steeled himself to say good-bye to his wife, and she sadly turned her horse for Brussels. Some miles ahead, the man who found Juana for him in Badajoz, John Kincaid, was again acting as host. Over a fire against the wall of Col. Barnard's cottage a huge camp kettle of tea, milked and sugared, stood ready for passing officers on the road: 'all the big-wigs of the army ... from the Duke downwards, claimed a cupful.'

Still the only supply vehicles at the front were either privately hired carriages or sutlers' carts. Sutlers were licensed freelance merchants; their extras – for those who could afford profiteers' prices – worked wonders to cheer up the 'withered pound of beef' the commissary doled out. Inside his cottage, Barnard had conjured another spread, 'a splendid breakfast' which Simmons shared. Young Leeke was roused by his servant and told that something was going on at his company; but after a mouthful of hot soup the tin was taken away with a 'Come, Master Leeke, I think you have had your share of that.' Leeke was too shy to argue. He had been intended by his mother for the Church, but stirring tales of the Spanish war set his heart on the army. Persuading his mother to write through family friends to Colborne, he got himself accepted for the crack 52nd, lodged his money as Ensign, took the coach to London to kit himself out, and a few days later, sword tangling his legs, landed damp and seasick at Ostend. He was as green as they come, but with a fatherly sergeant and sympathetic officers he settled in fast. Now his one anxiety was not to let his regiment down.

On the next hill beyond Leeke, Guards officers with money and enterprise had got up private comforts from Brussels. The young and dapper Gronow was gatecrashing: he should have

been with his own battalion in London. A couple of weeks ago, scenting battle, he had talked his way into a half-promised place on Picton's staff, borrowed £200, gambled and won £600, bought two thoroughbreds, slipped away without permission and taken the Ramsgate boat. Picton didn't need him but the 2/1st Guards, after a dressing-down, let him stay. Back now from sentry duty, he was greeted loudly by some friends and invited to the picnic breakfast: 'It will perhaps be your last.' Another called him over: 'Come here, Gronow, and tell us some London news.' Squatting under a couple of blankets, he was soon 'eating cold pie and drinking champagne'.

In rear of the left of line, 12th Light Dragoons had got wind of the abandoned supply wagons before Lambert's men got to work. A 'plundering expedition' returned laden, also with a present of 'cold beef, mutton, and veal' from an unusually generous sutler. Smith topped it off with as much brandy as he could swallow and, gorged and drowsy, was stretched on some straw beside the other officers when Uxbridge passed. The great man waved them back: 'Lie still, gentlemen, lie still, take all the sleep you can get ...'

$\mathscr{B}$ATTLE POSITIONS

Rue St Denis, Paris

More than a hundred miles south, the social and artistic capital of Europe was waking to a busy day. It was 8.30 a.m. in Paris, and a Parisian Sunday was as different from London's as were the cities themselves. In three weeks' time Mercer would feast his eyes on the fine evening view from Mont Valérien. 'Before us all Paris lay extended as in a plan . . . even the far-away country beyond,' he would write. Burning wood rather than coal, Paris had no London smoke-fog, but a 'light transparent vapour floating over the city'. He could pick out the soft outlines of the Column of Austerlitz, Notre Dame, the domes of the Panthéon and the Invalides, and 'in the distance . . . the smiling heights of Belleville . . . to the left . . . the steep slopes of Montmartre . . . the summit . . . with its . . . windmills and a telegraph . . .' Within the city Mercer, used to the 'dull avenues of brick and mortar' of London, found every street a revelation, the Boulevard des Italiens a world in itself.

A year ago the artist Haydon had coached from Dieppe, across an ocean of undulating green, league after league of young wheat and rye and barley, to be stunned by the 'hopeless confusion' of Paris. Narrow streets; foreigners; pretty girls,

Belleville

petticoats tucked up, darting between carts and carriages; life-size shop signs; noise; smells. This summer the uniforms had gone: no longer the pageant of the handsome Russian Guards-man, wasp-waisted, 'striding along like a giant ... the English officer, with his boyish face and broad shoulders; the heavy Austrian; the natty Prussian' that Haydon stared at. Paris was French now, and solidly anti-British. *'À bas les Anglais!'* the audience shouted, when Haydon attended a performance of *Hamlet*.

Living under strict censorship, the French were intelligent yet ignorant; for years Napoleon had muzzled all newspaper reports from abroad. Haydon found the French treated war as a normal state; the whole of a young man's life had been spent to the sound of drums. This Sunday morning, as the shutters were coming down in the street shops below, young Labretonnière, a maths student staying at the *Hôtel d'Anjou*, was shaken from sleep by loud explosions. He listened care-fully, then called excitedly to his room mate: 'Hippolyte ... the gun is firing from the Invalides. It must be a great victory!' Hurriedly dressing, they rushed to their local *Café des Pyrénées*. Wild with joy they devoured the official bulletin, and real-ized the guns were indeed signalling Napoleon's victory at Ligny. The regular booming brought back memories of other 'triumphs which had rocked our childhood'; 'intoxicated with pride', they looked to the future ...

Brussels was too near war to feel any romance today. Under a thick sky, rain lashed the hundreds of horses packed in the Place Royale and the tarpaulined carts jamming the streets. Talk everywhere was of whether to leave or not. The A.D.C., Basil Jackson, sent here to Headquarters from Waterloo yesterday, saw Prussian deserters looting, shops shuttered, wounded still in carts, even on the pavement.

Madame D'Arblay was woken at 6 a.m. by a violent knocking: all was lost; she must be at the wharf by eight, 'not a moment to lose!' Throwing her belongings into a bag, she and her maid set out on foot, jostled by crowds. Around the canal barge the throng was so thick she went to an inn to wait for tickets. But her friend rejoined her in despair: it was too late, all boats commandeered. With no carriage to be had, there was nothing for it but to return.

Among the crowds of military, Lt Ingilby, sent back at dawn from his Horse Artillery troop to find an escape route for Vivian's cavalry should it be needed, snatched a hasty breakfast in the *Hôtel d'Angleterre*. 'I carried off a cold fowl for the troop, who I knew had nothing.'

By 9 a.m., an Imperial breakfast served on silver plate was proceeding at *Le Caillou* farmhouse, south of Mont St Jean. Surrounded by Marshal Soult, Chief of Staff, and other generals, Napoleon ate silently. Not one to admit weakness, he hid the pain of piles and perhaps a fever under a brash display of confidence. Napoleon had never understood the achievements of Wellington's ragged army in far-off Spain; he despised British troops as much as British stupidity; but he had never himself met their red lines of infantry. On Elba, according to Col. Campbell, the British Commissioner, he called Wellington 'the first General in the world'; but if he meant it then he pretended the opposite now.

Napoleon changed on Elba: for the first time in his life he could seem pathetic, as when he appeared uninvited at a ball on the English frigate *Curaçoa*, sat alone without dancing, and hummed 'God Save the King' in time with the band at its end. Campbell reported his prisoner perpetually restless: 'he rides about and explores every hole and corner of the island till all his attendants are tired ... After dinner he will sometimes walk in his room for 2 or 3 hours together ...' But he ate well, and put on weight. An English visitor, J. B. Scott, couldn't believe the fat thighs and face so expressionless 'it appears even to indicate stupidity'; when the mask broke into a half-smile Scott found it charming, but his companions more like that of 'a clever, crafty priest'.

Today the Emperor was in no hurry. Already postponed from dawn, attack was now put back again until noon; to give, he explained, time for the ground to dry for his guns. Either no one told him Flanders clay would remain waterlogged far longer than that, or he simply could not summon the energy to

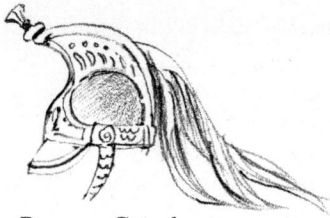

Dragoon Guards

Hussars

Light Dragoons

Greys

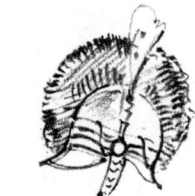

R.H.A.

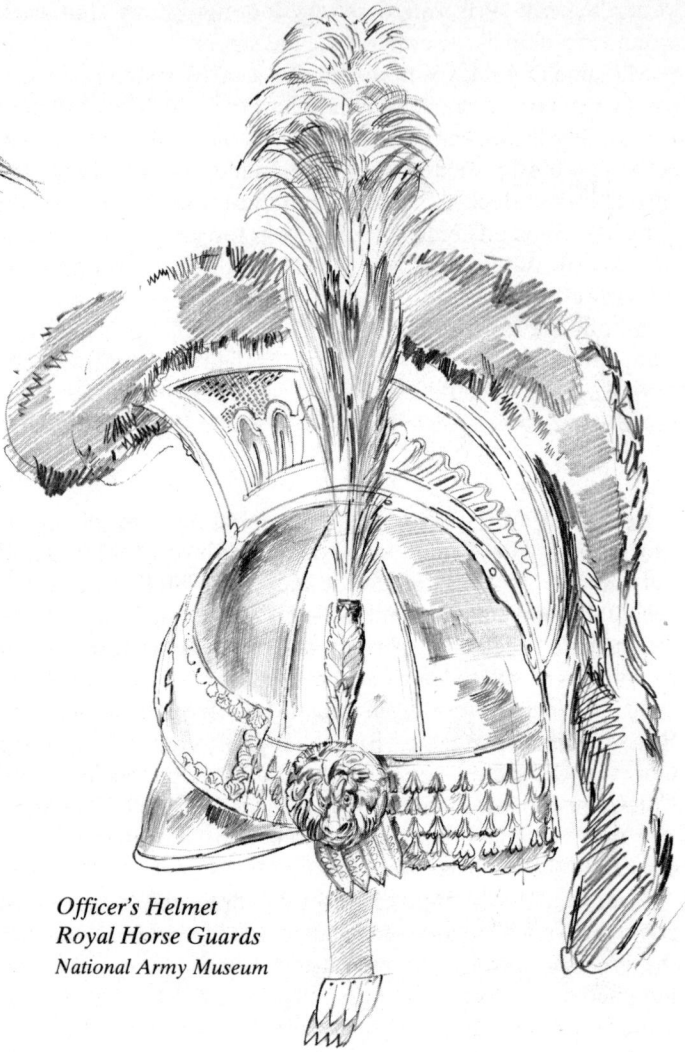

**Officer's Helmet
Royal Horse Guards**
National Army Museum

Rifles

Infantry

Highland

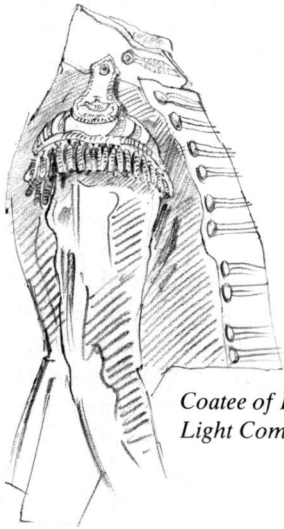

Coatee of Lt Anderson
Light Company 2/69th

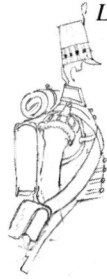

Light Infantry Shako

British Infantry Equipment:
Rolled blanket and pack on back.
Bayonet, haversack, waterbottle on left side.
Cartridge box on right.

Private's Coatee
Grenadier Guards

French
Infantry Shako

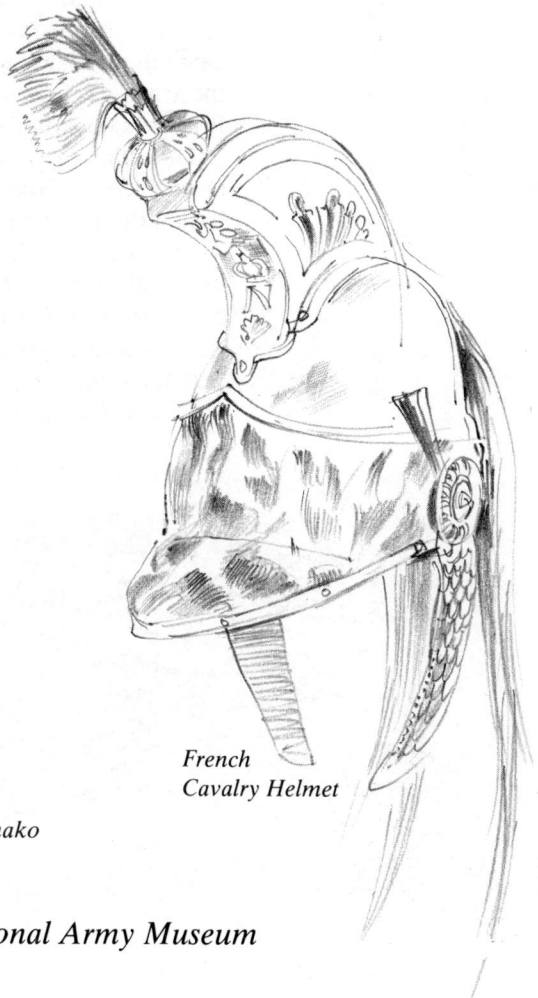

French
Cavalry Helmet

Uniforms in National Army Museum

command. His generals were worried, however. Soult, who respected the British and wanted Grouchy recalled, was taunted with his defeat in Spain by such a 'bad general' as Wellington. 'The odds are 9 to 1 in our favour,' Napoleon stated flatly. To Jerome's story of a planned Prussian link-up, he was contemptuous: Blücher could never regroup for at least two days after such a rout at Ligny.

This affair, he assured them, would be a walk-over. Meanwhile the battalions of the *Grande Armée* were steadily tramping up the roads from Fleurus and Quatre Bras. Long muddy columns passed *Le Caillou*, past the bivouacs of the Guard, towards the rise of the next ridge, where an inn named *La Belle Alliance* stood only 1,500 yards short of Wellington's main position. An order was issued to all units: the Emperor himself would review the whole army before battle was joined.

Things were getting more ship-shape in parts of Wellington's lines. About 9 a.m., says Kincaid, 95th were ordered to send all spare ammunition to a secure dump, and all baggage to the rear. As cartridge boxes were piled and wagons rumbled back along the road, everyone knew this meant retreat was finished; the army was to stand and fight. Word was out, too, that the Prussians were on their way.

Threading the bustle behind Mont St Jean, mail carts had arrived from Brussels. Black of the 3/1st wrote later to Exmouth: 'Dear Aunt, I received your letter on the field ...' Major Oldfield, with the Engineers at Waterloo, had just got 'the English mail' when an aide brought orders to entrench. To his horror he discovered that all his sappers had deserted; but a second order saved him; the Duke 'had given up the idea'.

In forward areas, the army was beginning to take preliminary positions. Out of a total force of rather more than 48,000 infantry now on the ridge, Wellington had only some 13,000 British and 3,200 King's German Legion. 2,275 British had

fallen at Quatre Bras; 2,396 were among the 15,000 infantry detached around Tubize; and Lambert's 2,567 seasoned veterans were still to arrive. All the rest, some 32,000, were foreign: Dutch-Belgian, Nassau, Hanoverian, Brunswick. And of the 13,000 British red-coats, more than half had never seen action. Cavalry was relatively strong, 14,000 odd, but again of all nations and largely untried.

To bolster weakness, foreign brigades were largely separated and placed with British divisions; within brigades themselves, experienced battalions were placed alongside raw. Across the main ridge, battalions were formed on a two-company frontage, and staggered in depth chequer-wise.

His inspection complete, Wellington halted with Muffling under a tall elm by the centre crossroads. The prominent landmark made a convenient command post from which aides could transmit and receive messages, wherever the Duke might be himself. His main concern now was how long Blücher would be. He himself could be under attack within the hour, and one Prussian corps on the field would be worth a whole army in Wavre. The French were also watching for the Prussians: Capt. Taylor from the furthest flank saw across the valley beyond Smohain 'a strong patrol of French Heavy Cavalry winding up a road . . . away to our left'.

The position long mapped and chosen was the best there was, but by no means perfect. No Spanish gorge made it near impregnable: southwards lay only a gentle rolling slope, shoulder high in wet corn, with dead ground hidden behind lesser ridges, before it rose to where the French were clearly forming a mile away. The Ohain cross road cut in the centre between awkwardly deep banks; to the rear the Brussels highway was fine for bringing up supplies but it also ran south, straight

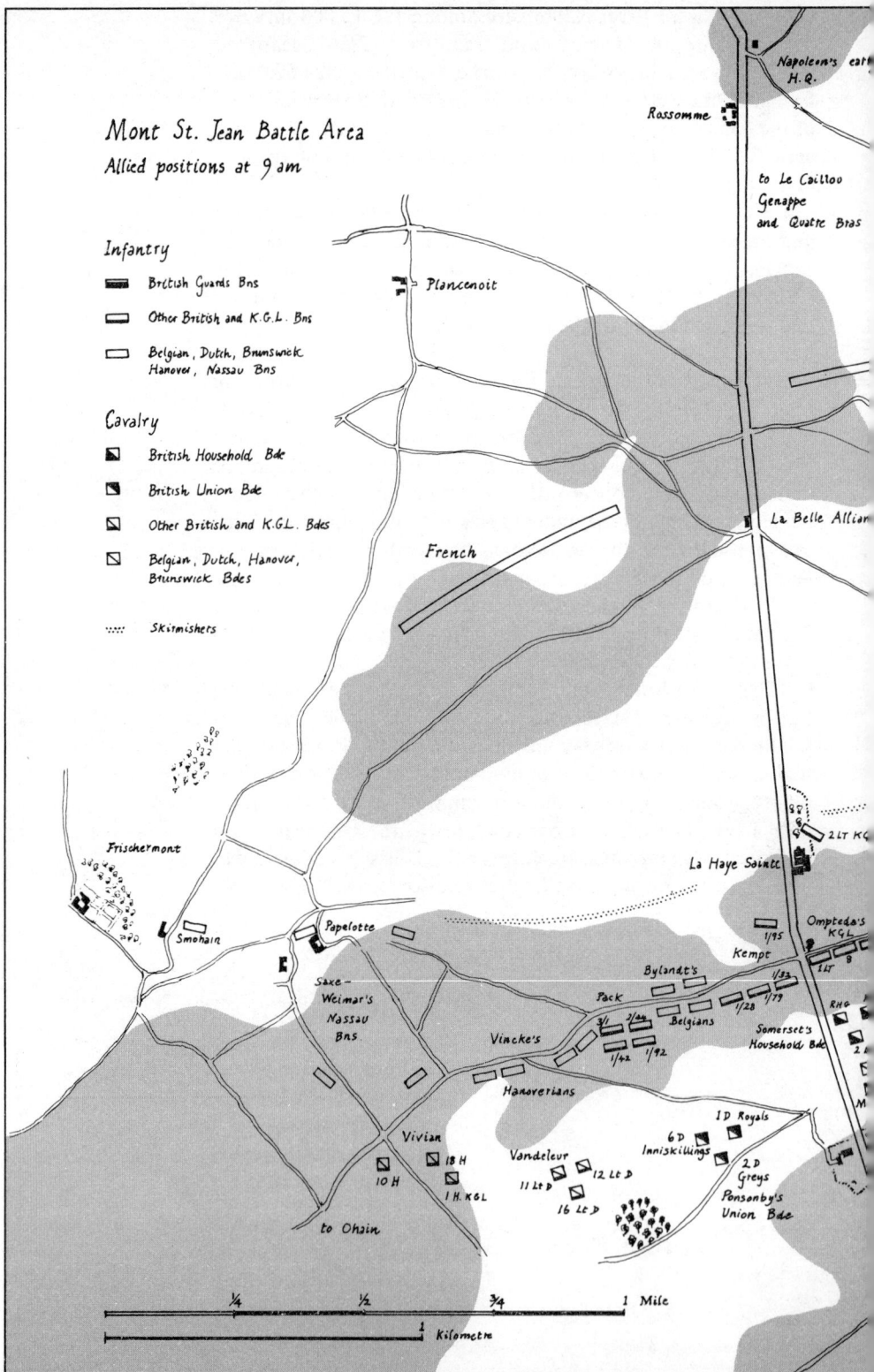

Mont St. Jean Battle Area
Allied positions at 9 am

Infantry

▬▬ British Guards Bns

▭ Other British and K.G.L. Bns

▭ Belgian, Dutch, Brunswick, Hanover, Nassau Bns

Cavalry

◼ British Household Bde

◼ British Union Bde

◻ Other British and K.G.L. Bdes

◻ Belgian, Dutch, Hanover, Brunswick Bdes

⋯⋯ Skirmishers

Plancenoit

Rassomme

Napoleon's earl[?] H.Q.

to Le Caillou Genappe and Quatre Bras

La Belle Alliance

French

Frischermont

Smohain

Papelotte

Saxe–Weimar's Nassau Bns

La Haye Sainte

2 Lt KGL

Ompteda's KGL

1/95

Kempt

Bylandt's

Pack

3/1 2/44 Belgians

1/42 1/92

1/32 1/79

1/28

Somerset's Household Bde

Vincke's

Hanoverians

Vivian

18 H

10 H

1 H. KGL

Vandeleur

11 Lt D 12 Lt D

16 Lt D

6 D Inniskillings

1 D Royals

2 D Greys

Ponsonby's Union Bde

to Ohain

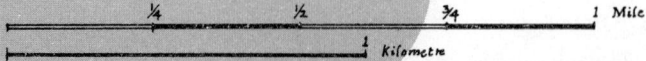

¼   ½   ¾   1 Mile

1 Kilometre

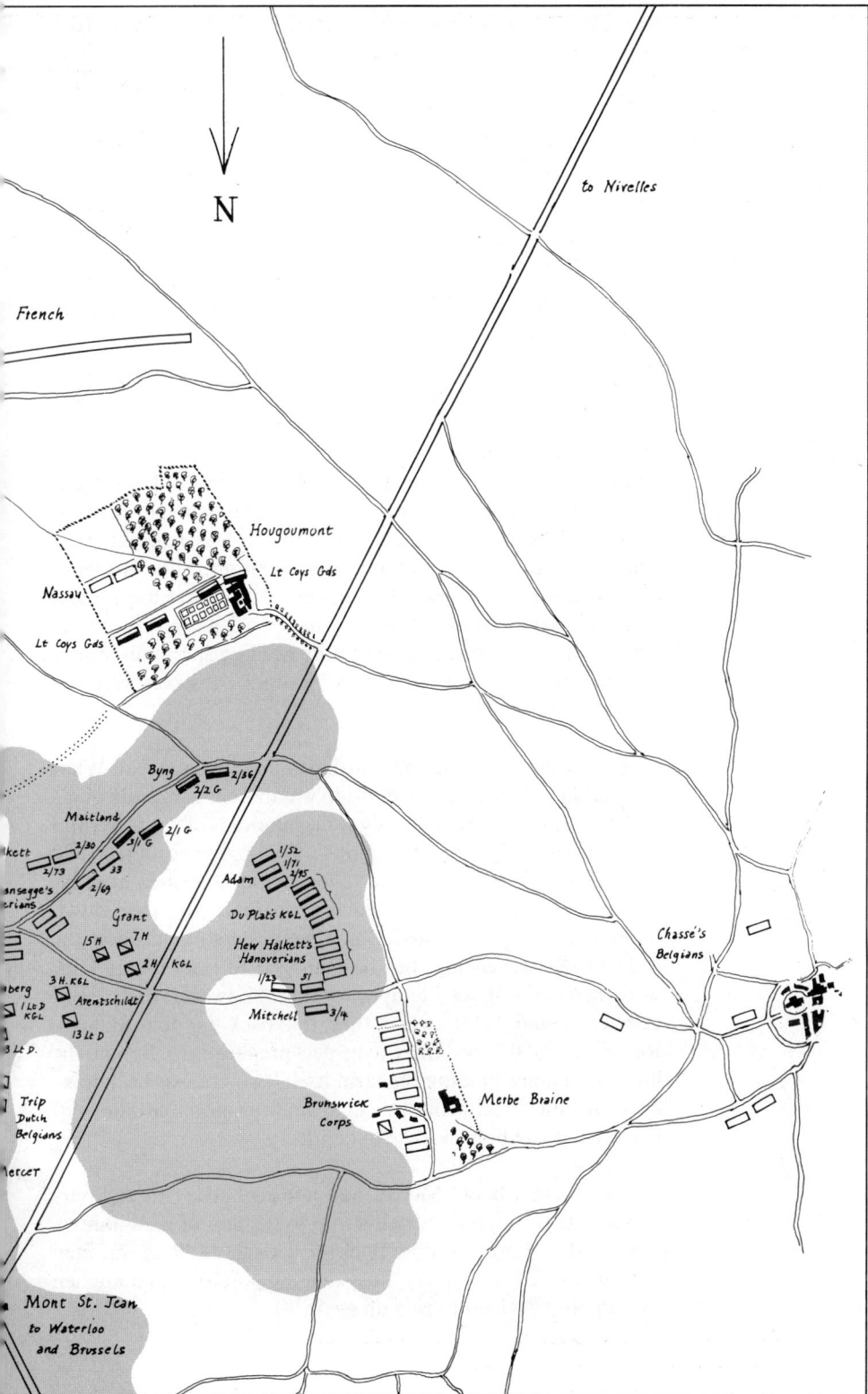

N

to Nivelles

French

Hougoumont

Lt Coys Gds

Nassau

Lt Coys Gds

Byng   2/3ᵈ
        2/2 G

Maitland   2/1 G
   2/30   3/1 G
...kett   33
2/73
...nsegge's   2/69
...erians
         Grant
   15ᴴ   7ᴴ
    2ᴴ   KGL

Adam   1/52
        1/71
        1/95

Du Plat's KGL

Hew Halkett's
Hanoverians
1/23   51

Chasse's
Belgians

3 H. KGL
...berg   Arentschildt
1 Lt D
KGL   13 Lt D

3 Lt D.

Mitchell   3/4

Merbe Braine

Trip
Dutch
Belgians

Brunswick
Corps

Mercer

Mont St. Jean
to Waterloo
and Brussels

as a die, between even deeper cuttings, making a dangerous approach road for Napoleon. The Nivelles fork came in absolutely unobstructed from the enemy's left, passing the rear of Hougoumont, which was itself half a mile forward of the main line. On the right flank, high ground projected beyond the road before swinging back almost at right angles to edge a shallow ravine towards Merbe Braine. Should the worst come, Soignes forest had plenty of paths as well as the main road through it northwards, but they were narrow and shut in by trees, difficult to defend. But, also to the rear, tracks radiated from Mont St Jean to all parts of the crest, able to carry reserves quickly under cover of a reverse slope to any threatened point.

Two farms lay in front of the line: Hougoumont, and a smaller one called La Haye Sainte which was only 300 yards down the Genappe road from Wellington's command post. Here Major Baring's 2nd Light Battalion, 376 men of the King's German Legion, had garrisoned the orchard, yard and rear garden. A main gate into the barn was missing, broken for firewood last night before its importance was realized; elsewhere the yard and its buildings were reinforced like Hougoumont's. Baring's Germans had Baker rifles, harder to ram and therefore with a slower fire rate than muskets, but more accurate. They also had a smaller bore needing special ammunition; each rifleman carried just sixty rounds – reserves were still with wagons to the rear.

Hougoumont, furthest forward, was first under threat. What looked like a whole French division was marching off side roads and beginning to assemble only some hundreds of yards beyond the furthest edge of its woods. Wellington ordered 300 Hanoverians and a Nassau battalion, some 1,000 men in all, to advance through the woods to their far end; and rode down himself to see them posted. Some youngsters panicked at the sight of massed enemy, but he managed to rally them. They were intended only as a temporary check, however; real all-out defence would begin when they fell back on the château. Returning, he stopped there to inspect preparations. Behind the light companies holding the farm itself, two Guards battalions lined the hill slope; behind them again four more battalions of II Division: a whole defence in depth.

Even further back, Mercer had left his battery three hours ago to ride through cavalry lines up to the rear of the infantry, but could find out nothing. Back with his guns, he set his men to follow Life Guardsmen 'busy digging potatoes' in a kitchen garden, and decided to ride up again.

Unknown to Mercer, his Chief, Col. Frazer, had left Waterloo and was watching wagons, spare limbers, field forges, rumble towards the front. Again he had his writing satchel out:

'June 18, quarter-past 9 a.m.

'All quiet on both sides, all getting into order. Ammunition ... coming up ... I expect we shall have some cannonading this afternoon. – Adieu for the present.'

At last some commissary wagons had reached the field. 92nd got rations at 9 a.m., says Lt Hope. He cut a steak 'from the hind quarter of a bullock', to grill on a ramrod. More spirits were issued, the regiment moved from its 'clay puddle' to firmer ground, and soon fresh fires were drying kilts and stockings. Some campaigners were even building huts.

At 9.30 a.m., six hours after dawn, a frail Blücher was still at Wavre, dictating a second letter to Muffling:

'Ill and old though I am, I shall nevertheless ride at the head of my troops to attack the enemy's right flank as soon as Napoleon makes any move against the Duke ...' Despite a late start, old 'Vorwärts' or 'Forwards' was ready for anything.

Gebhard Leberecht von Blücher, created 'Prince of Wahlstadt' in honour of his services, undisputed leader of the Prussian army, was almost completely uneducated save in farming and war. Staff work, detailed orders, plans, were left to Gneisenau, who really ran the army; but what Blücher could do, as none other, was to inspire his men. Wherever he chose to lead, they would follow.

As a hot-blooded Hussar officer he had drunk and gambled and survived one campaign after another throughout northern Europe. The bitter Napoleonic struggle which devastated Prussia left him with a deep hatred of the man, even of France: he could not forget the burning villages, the peasants murdered. Two years ago he led a cavalry charge to within 200 yards of killing the Emperor at Lutzen. He had lost a finger, limped from a fall twenty years ago, had a bullet-scarred back, and suffered from rheumatism, drink and the ravages of a rough life. Last year he seemed dying, with fever and bouts of madness. Badly trampled at Ligny, dosed that night with gin and reeking of garlic rubbed on his bruises, he had refused all ointment this morning. 'If things go well today,' he declared, stoutly buttoning his coat, 'we shall soon all be ... bathing in Paris.'

But Gneisenau added a secret footnote to Blücher's letter, asking Muffling to 'discover very carefully whether the Duke really meant to do battle ...' Suspecting Wellington, and preferring not to move at all, he had ensured a further delay. Although Bülow's corps – ordered to head the advance – had not been involved at Ligny and was fresh, it had furthest to march; until it cleared the road, others must wait.

If Blücher was late in joining Wellington, Grouchy was almost as late in pursuing Blücher. And not yet in the right direction: his two army corps, beginning now to snail along lanes and tracks, were heading more east than north, towards Perwez rather than Wavre. Napoleon hadn't helped, with no reply yet to Grouchy's night dispatch reporting progress.

Before 10 a.m., Napoleon had ridden forward to review his troops. Drums beating, eagles on high, regiment after regiment tramped by *La Belle Alliance*, crying 'Vive l'Empereur!' until the small hunched figure was left behind, as they branched off through fields to take post in a vast arc of strength. Away to the left, the lines of Reille's II Corps showed cavalry already across the Nivelles road and infantry before the Hougoumont woods; men of IV Corps were now taking the centre. Behind, more divisions: cavalry, infantry, artillery batteries and lastly the divisions of the Guard were massing forward in endless ribbons of men and animals. A wavering sun reflected now and again from steel, picking out through layers of mud the colour of splendid uniforms.

By such an imposing array it seemed Napoleon had hopes of scaring Wellington's foreign troops, especially pro-French Belgians, into desertion before a shot was fired. It seemed also to have taken his thoughts from Grouchy. Only at 10 a.m., he dictated a strangely confused reply: to continue pressing the rear of the Prussians, but also to join the main army as soon as possible. 'You will head for Wavre ...' But to reach the area of Mont St Jean via Wavre was making two sides of a triangle, miles and hours of needless marching ...

On the ridge opposite, 'About 10 ... Lord Hill, with his staff, came galloping along ... through the high corn ... as he passed ... he gave me one of his pleasantest smiles', which swelled young Leeke's pride and made up somewhat for his lost soup. Drums were beating the 52nd to arms. 'Nettles and I were warned by Winterbottom, the Adjutant, that we were to carry the colours.' Soon after, Kincaid spotted 'an unusual bustle ... among the staff officers', quickly followed by orders to stand to. German legion troops directly in front were moving over to the right; 95th now went forward to 'its fighting position'. Three advance companies lined a sandpit and knoll a little beyond the crossroads; remainder in two lines, one at the hedge, a second 100 yards back. Work parties began cutting trees and hauling branches for an abattis or barricade to block the Genappe road. All along the ridge, final adjustments: Wheeler's 51st manned a hillside above and behind Hougoumont.

Again Wheatley had time to stare. He wondered at the feelings of young Frenchmen, more upright, intelligent, civilized, he thought, than the 'heavy selfish Germans' of his regiment, and at the turn of fate which had made them enemies; by contrast he scorned a 'swelled-faced, ignorant booby, raw from England', cheek quivering in terror. Although near the boy a hardened, weather-beaten veteran, eyebrows blackened from powder flashes, also darted anxious glances towards the south.

'About 10,' the Legion ordered 'to clean out the muskets and fresh load ... Half an allowance of rum was then issued, and we descended into the plain ...' says Wheatley. Behind him now, he could see 'shoals of Cavalry' and, to his astonishment, the whole of the Horse Guards, whom he thought still in London at Knightsbridge Barracks.

From the Hussar lines, Surgeon Gibney noticed the day was fairing up. Head-tall crops were trampled flat to 'a sort of cake over the swamp', giving an open view of guns and wagons. All cavalry now marshalled: light squadrons, reconnaissance work mostly finished, protected each wing; two heavy brigades, Household and Union, astride the centre road. Uxbridge, riding the field with favourite aides from his own 7th Hussars, was suddenly faced by new worries. At the last moment he found he commanded foreign cavalry as well as British. Wellington had just told him, 'The Prince of Orange requests you will take charge ...' Stunned, he promised to do his best, but couldn't help saying it was 'unfortunate' he had never even met the officers.

By now the whole of five French army corps could be seen, displayed like a map. Wellington's staff were computing numbers; there must be 60 to 70,000 men in front – overwhelming odds given the doubtful quality of two thirds of the Allied army. The one hope was Blücher: if they had marched even at 8 a.m., let alone 'dawn', the Prussians couldn't be much longer. Skirmish fire was steadily growing, spreading.

On the extreme left flank, Capt. Taylor's heart suddenly leapt as horsemen in dark blue could be seen skirting some trees. It was a Prussian patrol. Its officer reined in and told him that Bülow, with 25,000 men, had reached Occey 'three quarters of a league distant'. Although the name wasn't on any map a junior officer instantly galloped to Uxbridge, who ordered Major Thornhill to carry the news straight to the Duke. Thornhill found Frazer following his horse artillery to the front, and

asked him to scribble a second copy. Riding on, Frazer met Picton, who told him an attack was imminent, 'the line was under arms'. Frazer stopped only to explain his battery positions and the site of ball cartridge reserves in the rear before continuing on towards the ridge. Skirmishers were now engaged all along the valley; around Hougoumont woods puffs of musket smoke floated across the untrodden corn.

Rain had stopped, and a hazy sun outlined distant hills. At moments bursts of music, perhaps cheering, were borne faintly on the breeze from the fantastic spectacle still unfolding on the opposite slopes. Except for the constant rattle of musketry, there was almost a pause. Most men were aware only of others nearby; but from the hill above Hougoumont one could see long blocks of red, white, blue, green, extending in mass for more than two miles, all the way to the extreme flank by Taylor's Hussars: the ranged battalions of an international army.

Not only staff officers assessed probabilities. Tomkinson, whose 16th Light Dragoons were the only cavalry to have ridden from Lisbon to the Pyrenees, cast an expert eye on the wet, heavy clay in front, which would slow any charge uphill, and on the open fields around Hougoumont which would make any surprise attack impossible.

The 1/95th, lining the edge of the crossroads, were some of the most experienced soldiers in the army. Superbly disciplined yet trained to act independently on outpost, crack shots with their Baker rifles, providing volunteers for the 'forlorn hope' to lead almost every assault, they knew their worth. Barnard, their Colonel, didn't believe in flogging; when a corporal was caught smuggling his wife into Ostend he silently approved when Simmons, acting as surgeon, stopped the sentence half-way through. Barnard was loved by his men; shot through the lungs at the Battle of Nivelles, he was carried back under fire by Simmons; when he rejoined three months later the whole regiment cheered.

Kincaid, their Scottish Adjutant, also knew the Peninsula. His bony frame and long nose hid a romantic heart; for two and a half years it beat for 'a young girl, dressed in white', seen once on a Lisbon balcony. He lost it again to Juana, Smith's bride, and to many a village siren – but not to two 6-foot women from the German Legion who overpriced a chicken, and who could have 'thrashed a better man than myself'. He admired his men – 'a more devoted set of fellows were never associated' – and he respected the French. 'Between us there was no humbug ... it was either peace or war.' In one retreat the boots had to be cut from his feet. Hardships brought rewards, though: after marching through twenty miles of rocky wilderness near Burgos, he came to the village of Arenas in the Ebro valley, 'one of the richest, loveliest ... spots ... I lay down that night in a cottage garden, with my head on a melon, and my eye on a cherry tree' and slept. He had lived through many battles, and led the storming party at Badajoz; but today as always, the 'certain sort of ... anxiety' chilled him as he waited.

Sgt Morris, returning diagonally up the ridge to the lines of the 2/73rd from La Haye Sainte, where he had gone for water, had seen something of battle lines forming. Shaved now and 'tolerably comfortable' in a clean shirt, he heard his brother had been ordered forward with a light company to join the skirmishers of the 95th. They shook hands, 'not supposing it likely that we should both be preserved through such a battle ...'

In the same brigade, Ensign Macready – unlike Morris – was almost completely inexperienced. He had said good-bye to his erratic theatre manager father a year before and joined the 30th Foot in Holland, but not till two days ago did he see the crows wheeling over his first battlefield at Quatre Bras. Today rations and drink came up by 11 a.m.; he had 'just stuck a ramrod through a noble slice of bull beef ... when an Aide-de-Camp came galloping up and roared out "Stand to your arms" ... our artillery arrived at full gallop ...' Lt Pratt, commanding a light company, got orders to 'show resistance against infantry' but if charged by cavalry to retire through the guns to the main body behind.

Frazer, who had been told that the Duke already knew about the Prussians, arrived near the 30th to find his artillery's reserve ammunition missing, and sent back a fast rider for the wagons. Gun batteries were forming now on forward slopes; teams of eight or nine men unhooking carriages, setting trails by handspikes, preparing ammunition and opening limbers, drivers taking horses to the rear. Light 6 and 9 pdr field guns fired a near-flat trajectory over open sights and needed positioning in front of infantry. Their range about 1,400 yards at 4 degrees elevation.

A horse artillery troop like Mercer's had six guns with limbers, in three divisions, each team drawn by eight horses and each with spare ammunition wagon drawn by six horses. Three additional ammunition wagons, spare wheel carriage, forge, baggage cart, all horse-drawn, and horses for officers and sergeant brought the total to 226 animals per troop.

Linstocks of burning hemp on spiked poles were stuck between each two guns; portfires were ready to transfer flame to barrel vents; gunpowder of saltpetre, sulphur and charcoal, already packed and weighed in cartridge bags; normal solid shot strapped to wooden sabots ready for ramming. Once loaded, charge bag was pricked open through the vent, then plugged with goose quill filled with powder. Other ammunition included canister and case, packing smaller bullets for close range; exploding shell with fuse; and spherical case or 'shrapnel' – named after the British inventor – giving air burst. Fuses were beechwood plugs, powder filled and cut to length needed: for 1,500 yards, time of flight was three seconds. Massive oak carriages on 5-ft wheels took recoil and were manhandled back after each round fired. The spongeman then swabbed out the barrel, reversed his staff and rammed a new cartridge and then a ball placed by the loader. Safe rate of fire, in smoke and excitement of action, not above two or three rounds per minute.

Orders today forbade counter-battery fire. In a day-long battle brass barrels could overheat and droop; Wellington wanted every piece and every round to be used against infantry and cavalry only. When charged, gunners to fire until the last moment before running for shelter back to main line.

Amid a stream of messages, Wellington was stationed now behind Hougoumont. An attack was clearly coming here, but it might be a feint. An oddly delayed letter, dated the 15th, was handed him, relaying secret reports from spies that French officers expected 'a battle within three days'. Wellington, perhaps ironically, signed it nevertheless: 'Received from Grant.

9 Pdr Gun and Carriage

Lifting Handles and Trunnions

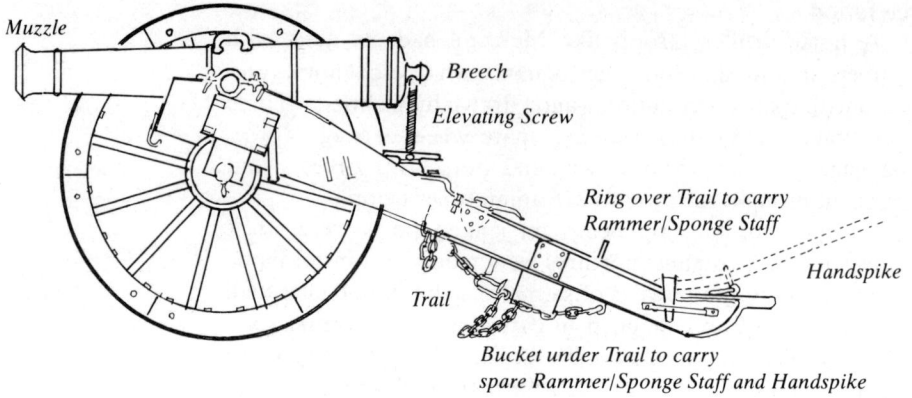

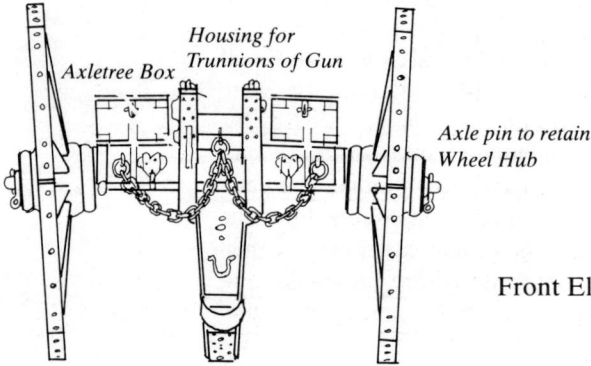

Muzzle

Breech

Elevating Screw

Ring over Trail to carry
Rammer/Sponge Staff

Handspike

Trail

Bucket under Trail to carry
spare Rammer/Sponge Staff and Handspike

Housing for
Trunnions of Gun

Axletree Box

Axle pin to retain
Wheel Hub

Front Elevation of Carriage

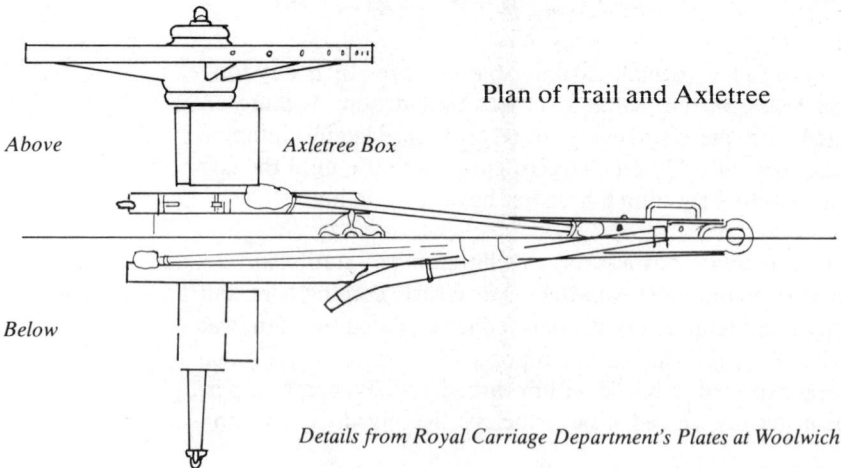

Plan of Trail and Axletree

Above

Axletree Box

Below

Details from Royal Carriage Department's Plates at Woolwich

Infantry Tower Musket (Brown Bess)

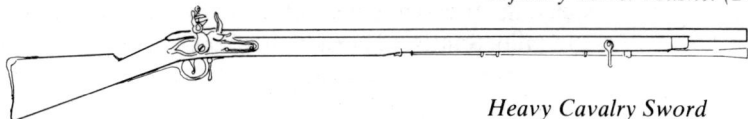

Heavy Cavalry Sword

Infantry Halberd

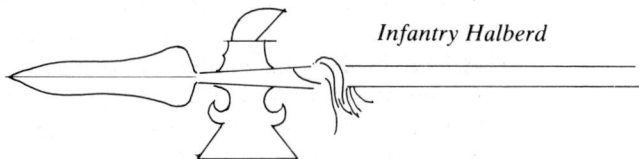

Light Cavalry Sword

Infantry Spontoon

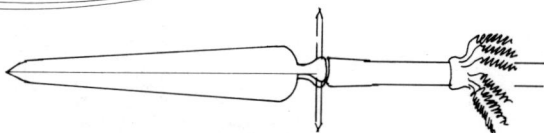

Cavalry Pistol
National Army Museum

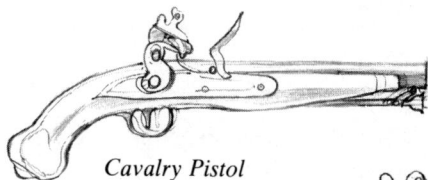

Baker Rifle
National Army Museum

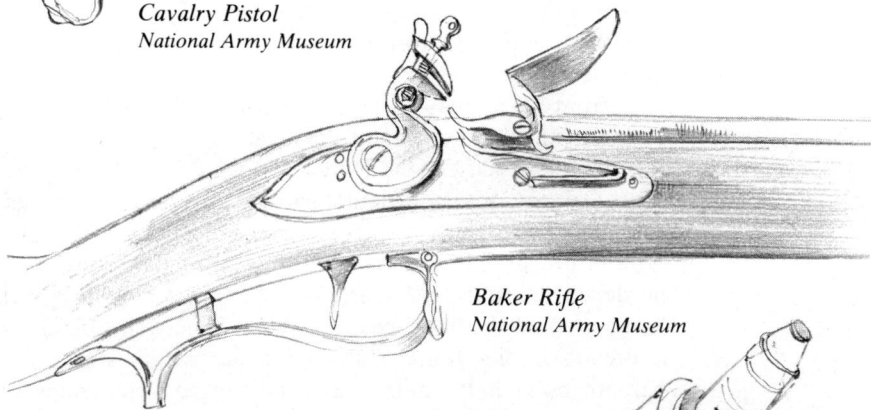

Rifleman's Powder Horn
National Army Museum

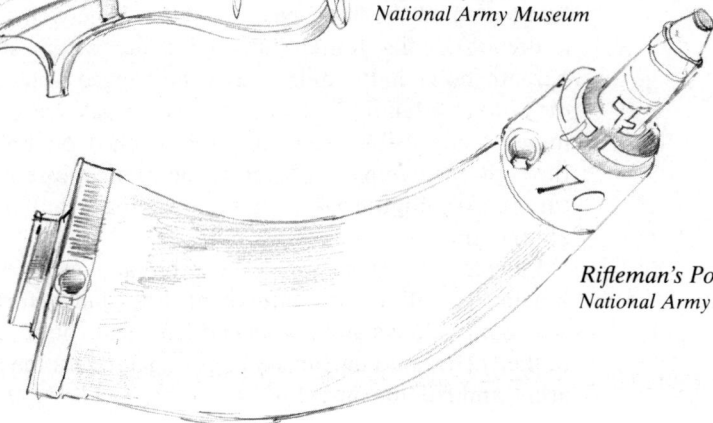

June 18. 11 a.m.' A lean, dusty rider coming up fast was more welcome. It was Harry Smith.

'Hallo, Smith, where are you from last?'

'From General Lambert's Brigade, and they from America ... and very strong.'

He overheard an aide doubting that the French were in earnest. Wellington snapped back, 'Nonsense. Their columns are already forming ...' He turned to Smith, ordering him to halt his brigade at the Nivelles road fork and await further orders – probably to reinforce Picton's left.

Lambert's Brigade were true veterans. Nine long years since Sgt Lawrence, now twenty-four, had run away from a boyhood apprenticeship in Dorset, and with 7s. in his pocket escaped into the 40th Ft. He carried a ball in his knee and scars on his back from 175 lashes – part sentence for walking off guard duty once. He knew the vermin of Portugal and the rocks of Spain. Storming party at Ciudad Rodrigo; several wounds; service in New Orleans; return Atlantic voyage diverted by a frigate carrying news of fresh war in Flanders, direct to Ostend without sight of England: he knew all about the army. His body was so hardened he couldn't sleep on a bed in Spain; a kind host found him curled on the floor. Near Toulouse he gave his blanket to a French soldier found shot and dying within sight of his parents' home half a mile away, who begged to be dragged to die among a family he had never seen in six years; but battle made it impossible. A tame cock perched on his knapsack through one campaign. After seeing him capture a mountain cannon, Wellington asked his name, saying 'I shall think of you another day'.

Lawrence and the rest of the brigade were thinking of practically nothing at the moment. Fifty miles' forced march through two days and nights had left them robots. Lt Drewe, of the 1/27th, said his Inniskillings staggered off the road, piled arms, and fell 'unconscious'.

Some Inniskillings were still ninety miles away, off Ostend. The rain storm was over the Channel coast by now, roughening seas, keeping *Sharpshooter* convoy still hove-to. Bakewell's diary: 'the wind ... so violent that the Bote which was selected to fetch us on to the shore, thought it not safe to approach ...' Best part of one and a half battalions of seasoned infantry would never reach Waterloo until battle was over.

At least one visitor, staying with his wife and family, was braving the rain in Brussels. Thomas Creevey wrote: 'Between 11 and 12 I perceived the horses, men, carts and carriages ... laden with baggage ... had received orders to march.' He waited anxiously to see which route they would take – the Antwerp or the Ostend road would mean retreat. Overjoyed, he saw 'they all went up the Rue de Namur *towards the army*'.

And nine miles from Wellington, Blücher and staff were riding out from Wavre. Ahead of them, Bülow's men were slowly ploughing through sunken lanes.

Along the Mont St Jean ridge, excitement had died to gnawing fear and doubt. One unspoken question lay behind every thought: will I be alive tomorrow? Soldier Tom took the oath

the same year as Sgt Lawrence. Tall and handsome, the favourite son of a poor family who had hoped he would become

ORDER OF BATTLE 18 JUNE 1815

ALLIED ARMY. Strengths of officers and men, with people quoted in text:
Commander-in-Chief: Field Marshal the Duke of Wellington
Corps Commanders: The Prince of Orange and Lt-General Lord Hill
Deputy Quartermaster General: Col. Sir William Delancey (A.D.C. Basil Jackson)

INFANTRY

1st British Division (Cooke)		
Maitland's Bde.	2/1 Guards (Gronow)	29 + 752
	3/1 Guards (Dirom)	29 + 818
Byng's Bde.	2/2 Guards Coldstream (Bowles, Short)	36 + 1,006
	2/3 Guards (Clay)	34 + 1,021
2nd British Division (Clinton)		
Adam's Bde.	1/52 Oxfordshire (Leeke)	59 + 1,079
	1/71 Glasgow Highlanders (Tom)	50 + 931
	2/95 Rifles 6 Coys (Lewis)	34 + 621
	3/95 Rifles 2 Coys	10 + 193
Du Plat's Bde.	King's German Legion 4 Line Bns	118 + 1,890
Hew Halkett's Bde.	Hanoverian Landwehr troops	2,454
3rd British Division (Alten)		
Colin Halkett's Bde.	2/30 Cambridge (Macready)	40 + 593
	1/33 West Riding	31 + 535
	2/69 South Lincoln	30 + 511
	2/73 Highland (Morris)	23 + 475
Ompteda's Bde.	K G L 1st 2nd Lt Bns (Graeme)	63 + 864
	5th, 8th Line Bns (Wheatley)	63 + 984
Kielmansegge's Bde.	Hanoverian Regulars	3,189
4th British Division (Colville)		
Mitchell's Bde.	3/14 Buckinghamshire (Keppel)	38 + 592
	1/23 Royal Welch Fusiliers	44 + 697
	1/51 Second West Riding (Wheeler)	45 + 474
Johnstone's Bde. (not at Waterloo)		
Lyon's Bde. Hanoverian (not at Waterloo)		
5th British Division (Picton)		
Kempt's Bde.	1/28 North Gloucester	35 + 521
	1/32 Cornwall (Ross-Lewin)	26 + 477
	1/79 Cameron Highlanders (Douglas)	26 + 414
	1/95 Rifles (Barnard, Kincaid, Leach, Simmons)	17 + 401
Pack's Bde.	3/1 Royal Scots (Black)	36 + 417
	1/42 Royal Highlanders – Black Watch (Anton)	17 + 312
	2/44 East Essex	20 + 450
	1/92 Gordon Highlanders (Hope, Robertson)	22 + 400
Vincke's Bde.	Hanoverian Landwehr troops	2,514
6th British Division (Cole – absent on leave)		
Lambert's Bde. (A.D.C. Harry Smith)	1/4 King's Own	669
	1/27 Inniskilling	698
	1/40 Somerset (Lawrence)	761
	2/81 (detached)	
Best's Bde.	Hanoverian Landwehr troops	2,582
1st Netherlands Division (Stedman) (not at Waterloo)		
2nd Netherlands Division (Perponcher)		
Bylandt's Bde.	Jaegers and Militia	3,233
Saxe-Weimar's Bde.	Nassau Regulars	4,300
3rd Netherlands Division (Chassé)		
Ditmer's Bde.	Jaegers and Militia	3,088

Aubremé's Bde.	Regulars and Militia	3,581
Brunswick Corps	(8 Bns of German regulars)	5,376
Nassau Bde.	(Kruse) 3 Bns of Nassau regulars	2,880

CAVALRY (The Earl of Uxbridge commanding)

Somerset's Household Bde.	1st Life Guards (Haddy James)	16 + 229
	2nd Life Guards (Waymouth)	20 + 215
	Royal Horse Guards – Blues	19 + 232
	1st King's Dragoon Guards	29 + 568
Ponsonby's Union Bde.	1st Dragoons – Royals	30 + 398
	2nd North British – Scots Greys (Dickson)	28 + 414
	6th Dragoons – Inniskilling	26 + 419
Dornberg's Bde.	1st Lt Dragoons K G L	34 + 500
	2nd Lt Dragoons K G L	33 + 472
	23rd Lt Dragoons (Grove)	28 + 313
Vandeleur's Bde.	11th Lt Dragoons	27 + 408
	12th Lt Dragoons (Hay, Smith)	26 + 401
	16th Lt Dragoons (Tomkinson)	30 + 403
Grant's Bde.	2nd Hussars K G L (detached)	
	7th Hussars (Elphinstone, Verner)	18 + 344
	15th Hussars (Dalrymple, Gibney)	28 + 419
Vivian's Bde.	1st Hussars K G L	36 + 550
	10th Hussars (Taylor)	26 + 426
	18th Hussars (Duperier)	25 + 417
Arentschildt's Bde.	3rd Hussars K G L	37 + 647
	13th Lt Dragoons	28 + 420
Estorff's Bde.	Hanoverian. Cumberland, Prince Regent's, Bremen and Verden Hussars	1,682
Trip's Bde.	Dutch and Belgian Carabiniers	1,237
Ghigny's Bde.	4th Dutch Lt Dragoons	647
	8th Belgian Hussars	439
Merlen's Bde.	5th Belgian Lt Dragoons	441
	6th Dutch Hussars	641
Brunswick Cavalry	2nd Hussars 1 Squadron Uhlans	912

ARTILLERY (Col. Sir George Wood commanding)

Royal Horse Artillery (Lt-Col. Sir Augustus Frazer commanding)

Six troops of 6 guns. Bull's (Howitzers), Webber Smith's Gardiner's, Whinyates's (all 6 pdrs, Whinyates's with rockets), Mercer's, Ramsay's (both 9 pdrs)	36 guns
Dutch Horse Artillery. Two half-troops of Petter and Gey	8 guns
Royal Horse Artillery reserve. Ross's (9 pdrs), Beane's (6 pdrs)	12 guns
Field Batteries attached to infantry divisions	
Royal Artillery. Sandham's, Bolton's, Lloyd's, Sinclair's, Roger's (all 9 pdrs); Brome's and Unett's (not at Waterloo)	30 guns
K G L. Kuhlmann's, Cleeve's, Sympher's	18 guns
Hanoverian. Rettberg's and Braun's	12 guns
Dutch Belgian. Byleveld's, Stievenaar's, Krahmer's, Lux's	32 guns
Brunswick. Heinemann's and Moll's	16 guns

Approximate total strengths on field, all ranks:

Allied Army. 50,003 infantry, 14,738 cavalry, 5,515 artillery, 164 guns, 1,352 R.E. and services

Prussian Army (marching from Wavre). 60,000 infantry, 9,000 cavalry, 9,000 artillery, engineers and services, 260 guns

French Army (right wing under Grouchy on march to Wavre).
left wing (Ney). 50,000 infantry, 15,000 cavalry, 10,000 artillery, engineers and services, 266 guns

a clergyman, at sixteen he had insisted on cutting adrift to try his luck as an actor. But struck dumb with stage-fright, he was hissed off the stage, and too ashamed to return home, he embarked at Leith for the Glasgow Highlanders. 'You are a noble lad, and shall be an officer,' said the crafty sergeant. He had left his parents in tears, but during nine years' service had never managed to see them since. A recruit, as raw as Tom was once, confessed today, 'Tom, you are an old soldier ... and have every chance to escape ... I am sure I am to fall ...' Nothing could console the boy, and Tom, who could write, promised to send a message to his parents should he die.

One battalion, the 3/14th Buckinghamshire, was nearly all boys, with fourteen officers and 300 privates under twenty, mostly 'fresh from the plough', says Keppel – only sixteen himself. Their appearance on parade in Brussels was so bumpkin-like that Col. Tidy had to argue hard to have them sent on active service at all.

One of the stoutest hearts in the battalion was female. Mrs Ross had followed her man – then in the 95th – in every battle; she was wounded in Buenos Aires; again today she refused to leave the field. Her husband had been promoted to Quartermaster, however, and Col. Tidy explained that 'what was right and proper in a sergeant's wife, was not so becoming in an officer's lady'. Pride appealed to, she retired to a bird's-eye view from a belfry.

Lying near, in the same brigade, Sgt Wheeler had seen one wife widowed three times in five months, each time taken on by another man for her cooking. For his part, he stayed single. 'No doubt there are many sweets in having a pretty young woman for a comrade, but ... there is an infinite number of bitters ... a soldier should always be able to say when his cap is on, his family is covered; then he is as free as air.' Wheeler had no illusions about today. 'The best way is to enjoy ourselves while we can, it will be time to bid the Devil good morning when we meet him ... no doubt there will be hot work ahead ...'

One of Wellington's toughest commanders was Welsh, Sir Thomas Picton. A lifetime's experience had taught him the highest regard for British soldiers – and French officers. 'If I had 50,000 such men as I commanded in Spain, with French officers at their head, I'm damned if I wouldn't march from one end of Europe to the other.' As for British officers, 'Why, damn it, where is their military education? where our military schools and colleges? ... Our fellows ... know nothing. We are saved by our N.C.O.s, who are the best in the world.' So heard an astounded Gronow, crossing with Picton to Ostend, and himself hoping for a staff appointment.

Picton had strange premonitions. In England he had told his friends this campaign would be his last. He wound up his affairs, and once, in a churchyard, he jumped into a freshly-dug grave and, stretching himself full-length, laughed, 'Why, I think this would do for me.'

One officer in Picton's division had met Napoleon on Elba. Col. Douglas, of the 79th Cameron Highlanders, had to explain to a fascinated Emperor that Scottish regiments really did wear the kilt, but he had none with him to show. Napoleon chatted about Spain: 'Your soldiers had plenty to drink there ...' Then the kilt again: 'The 48th also wear the kilt?' 'No, Sire, the 42nd.' The great man at length, with 'a long and low bow', rode on, leaving Douglas probably the only man on the ridge today whom Napoleon had raised his hat to.

Wellington, still behind Hougoumont, could see the French advancing now in earnest; skirmishers of both sides were firing heavily. In his career, he had countered every kind of attack; no one could match his uncanny sense for detecting a future point of danger. The complete corps now ranged against his right seemed in earnest, but French gun teams were beginning to draw out along a ridge westwards, battery after battery, some eighty guns in all, soon extending all the way to the Genappe road and making too wide an arc to be aligned against Hougoumont alone.

Wellington's tested method of defence was simple but flexible: to shelter his infantry, already formed, behind cover; to pulverize any attack with artillery fire until the last moment; then suddenly to bring forward double lines of infantry firing massive controlled volleys; finally to complete any rout with cavalry or bayonet. He had criticized British cavalry's wild charges, but the superb fire discipline of his resolute infantry had won time and again.

The infantryman's weapons remained the old 'Brown Bess', a long 42-inch barrel, ¾-inch bore musket, loaded and rammed like a gun. Each cartridge held powder and ball in a sewn packet. The firer bit off the top of the paper cartridge, shook some powder in the pan and the rest down the barrel, dropped in the ball and then rammed the cartridge bag after it to make a tight wad. Smooth bore and loose fit gave accuracy only to about 75 yards, but the heavy 1-oz ball would go on to penetrate three-inch solid oak at 200. Musket and bayonet weighed some 11 lb. Damp powder or failure of flint to spark caused frequent misfires; rate of fire was from three to six rounds per minute according to skill and care in aiming. Given miss-hits and failures, effective stopping power needed a concentrated volley from men firing shoulder to shoulder, in two or three lines; but since a resolute enemy could do a lot in the ten to twenty seconds between shots, firing was by alternate companies or platoons, thus giving each group time to reload.

In all armies infantry worked best in line, where each man, even if raw and half-trained, felt the support of others close beside him, rear ranks replacing casualties. Except on the march, even an advancing column was really a succession of lines at varying intervals. Ahead of these, skirmishers, acting in pairs, delayed or spearheaded an advance by harassing fire before joining their main lines. Against cavalry, which could

simply ride it down, however, a line must form a four-deep square with hedged bayonets, front ranks kneeling. But dense squares were terribly vulnerable to artillery.

Across the valley, Napoleon had issued final battle orders. Before a massive main drive on Mont St Jean, Prince Jerome's division, on the far left of Reille's Corps, would divert attention from the centre by capturing the prominent woods and house of Hougoumont. A divisional battery of long 12 pdr guns was aligned, ready.

The rattle of rifle and musket fire was suddenly shaken by the echo of a gun. Before smoke had drifted clear, the French battery was firing. Leeke, lying with the 52nd, 300 yards from the crest, remembered 'Exactly at 12 o'clock by Chalmers's watch'; Lord Hill, with a stop watch, recorded 11.50.

Everyone was suddenly alert. Macready threw off 'a wet blanket I had wrapped around me, gave myself a shake ...', the 'sort of chill and rising sensation' in his heart suddenly snapped.

All along the rear of the crest drums and bugles were sounding the call to arms. Simmons: 'formed columns (not for Prayers ...)' Further back and to each flank, cavalry was roused. Hay's 12th Light Dragoons ordered, 'Bridle up and stand up to your horses!'

13

CHÂTEAU DE HOUGOUMONT

By Hougoumont, Clay and his comrades of 2/3rd Guards were cutting fire pits in the orchard hedge when they were ordered around the buildings to a long kitchen garden on the west side, overlooking open fields. Already the high corn was waving as hidden skirmishers advanced astride the Nivelles road. Musket balls whined overhead, striking Clay's shoe heels as he hugged the ground. Twisting his head, he could just see Col. Hepburn 'on his charger' watching from the higher road behind. Noise of skirmishers and the crash of gunfire in the trees to the south sounded nearer. British batteries opened first ranging shots.

From higher slope, forward officers saw the first shell, from Cleeve's Battery, burst in the middle of a French column. Macready with his light company was ordered further downhill to protect the guns, now firing overhead. He could see the steady lines converging on Hougoumont wood, and in the far distance the red of French lancers.

A group of horsemen was well in advance of the line, where Wellington sat watching quietly, intently. In plain civilian clothes – blue cape, comfortable coat and breeches – writing materials for orders in a saddle bag, his whole presence radiated efficiency. His only decorations four cockades, for Britain, Spain, Portugal and the Netherlands, in his hat. All careful planning was over: he faced now the old test he knew too well;

the exhausting strain of continual command decisions, of instant reaction to the slightest change of circumstances, hour after hour through noise and confusion of actual battle. And this battle would settle the fate of France, Belgium, Europe, for generations. With the hotch-potch army he had, he knew the whole weight of responsibility lay on him alone. Courage, steel nerves and self-discipline from a life-time's soldiering helped; above all, to meet the supreme task of inspiring others by example, he was forced to a complete disregard for his own safety.

Musketry swelled to a muffled roar as enemy troops drove into the southern wood. Nassau defenders were retreating, but clearly resisting strongly. Muffling was worried about Hougoumont itself. Wellington reassured him of the quality of the Coldstream commander there, saying, 'Ah, you don't know Macdonell. I've thrown Macdonell into it.' Muffling worried too about the open hedges bordering the Nivelles road, and Wellington ordered Belgians to move in from far right, and British reserves from rear. First one company, then three others, including Wheeler's, of 51st 'ordered down' from their hill; in time to see swarms of Lancers on the road.

Despite heavy loss, French infantry in strength was smashing through the wood fast; almost at top northern boundary by now. Clay's light company was under heavy fire: as shouts and drums beating the '*pas de charge*' sounded through the corn in front, it got the 'expected signal' to retire to the farm, to avoid being cut off. To delay enemy skirmishers, Ensign Standen led a section of the company in a charge. Clay and a friend dropped behind a haystack near the south gate to give covering fire, exchanging shots with French now hidden in the hedge, reloading and firing as fast as they could until they realized they were on their own; their company back inside the farm.

Three quarters of a mile away, Capt. Verner in the 7th Hussars had already heard the 'unmistakable' roll of musketry. Shot from French batteries, firing uphill, was passing clear over the crest and landing among them. As they moved out of line

of fire a man beside Verner was suddenly crushed through the chest. Sgt-Major Edwards turned roughly to his wife: 'What's the matter with you, are you afraid?' The troop captain discovered that the wife, on a small pony, was still with the regiment; asking sharply if she was expected 'to go into action', he had her sent back.

In a direct line with Clay and Verner but well out of gun range, Mercer's teams stood harnessed in 'one unbroken solitude'. Besides worrying about a battle beginning without him, he spared a sigh for wasted soup; some bright gunner had emptied the kettle before hanging it under an ammunition wagon. At least his dog, Bal, was with him – companion through eleven years and the whole North American campaign. Out of the blue, a sign of life: 'a fine tall upright old gentleman, in plain clothes, followed by two young ones' coming 'across our front at a gallop' towards the right. Unknown to Mercer, the Duke of Richmond.

More French guns were firing; stray shots striking the crossroads. Kincaid: 'a cannon ball, too, came from the Lord knows where ...' Simmons: 'singled out a man in the rear rank of the rear company and smashed his head to pieces. Some men of a red regiment were cutting up a bullock for rations ... this shot started them off to their corps.' Simmons was not Yorkshire for nothing. The meat looked so good he sent his servant to cut a chunk, bury it and mark the hole for later. His men laughed and 'Sir Andrew shook his head at me', but serious business interrupted: he took a working party to cut more wood for the road barricade near La Haye Sainte. As British batteries opened, he stared at some raw German troops 'so alarmed that they blunderingly crossed in front of the guns', escaping death by inches.

On the main road behind, Frazer met Uxbridge who gave him 'free use' of all horse artillery batteries attached to cavalry. He at once sent for Bull's Troop, and watched with pride the glossy horses and expert drill of the six heavy $5\frac{1}{2}$-inch howitzer teams as they galloped up, 'their very appearance' heartening the Guards Brigade lying on the open slope. Wellington joined him, explaining that he wanted air burst over the southern half of Hougoumont woods, but warned him of the British troops fighting in the northern fringe. 'Colonel Frazer, you are going to do a very delicate thing; can you depend upon the force of your howitzers?' Frazer reassured him; together they watched fuses cut to 4th notch – for two seconds burning time – for 1,000

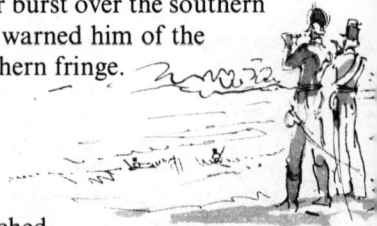

yards range, the careful sighting by numbers one over their barrels, the first salvo exploding perfectly beyond the tree tops. Wellington ordered back some Guards officers who had strolled across to watch; 'they would have the devil's own fire upon them immediately.' Within minutes, Bull's teams, firing steadily, came under heavy shelling from twelve French 9 pdrs in front and four from a flank. Frazer rode further right, and decided to strengthen the gun line there with Mercer's and Ramsay's Troops.

Exposed ridge around Wellington was no place for tourists. One of the boys Mercer saw ride up was fifteen-year-old William Lennox, with a broken arm and one eye out from a bad fall weeks ago, dismissed as unfit when he reported just now as one of General Maitland's A.D.C.s. Amid noise of British guns and the whirr and hiss of French bullets and cannon balls, Lennox's father, the Duke of Richmond, although civilian now, had a soldier's ideas on education. He rode up firmly to his son: 'I'm glad to see you stand fire so well.'

Well to the rear was almost worse. Shot and shell, sailing high over the crest, was exploding and plunging in the fields, leaving only a narrow strip of dead ground immediately below the ridge untouched. Leeke had his head on his company colour-sergeant's knapsack, trying to doze, when a 'rattle against the mess tins' inches from his face had him wide awake. Sgt Rhodes held out a shell fragment half the size of his hand: 'If that had hit either you or me on the head, Sir, I think it would have settled our business for us.'

Over by the centre road, Morris and two men from each company were getting salt provisions and spirits for the 2/73rd. Standing in a queue for the wagons, he saw a tall Life Guardsman drinking heavily the 'raw spirit'. The man was pointed out as the famous prizefighter Shaw, who had challenged all England on Hounslow Heath two months ago.

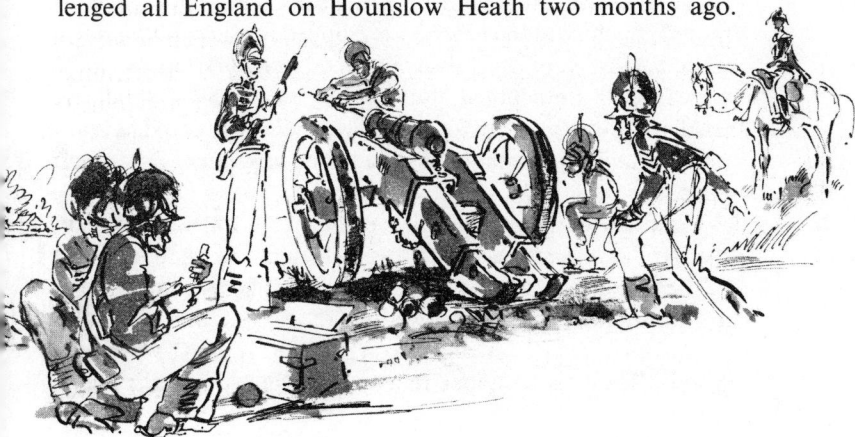

Morris got his gin just in time; 'a cannon-shot went through the cask'. Since three canteens were to be kept aside for wounded, Morris and Sgt Burton took 'an extra drop' together and decided to keep some back. Morris wondered if they would be alive to enjoy it, but his pal had an old soldier's faith: 'Tom, I'll tell you what it is; there is no shot made yet for either you or me.'

The roar increased. Over the hill, French attackers had pushed right through the woods, cutting their way with an axe through the last defended hedge, rushed a half-field but despite desperate bravery were thrown back from the high-loopholed wall bordering orchard and garden. Leaving their fallen thick on the ground, Jerome's men finally retreated. A pause; then redoubled artillery fire signalled another attack. This time men from Foy's division as well. They drove everything before them across the eastern orchard to a sunken road at the far edge. The walled garden held, but west of it another assault, cutting off Clay, surged down the side of the buildings and round to the rear entrance. A giant French lieutenant hacked with an axe at an exposed part of the gates' cross beam until a massed rush burst it open. In slippery mud and thick smoke savage hand-to-hand fighting spread across the yard; Standen's company was driven into stables, sheds, into the farmhouse itself, firing from parlour windows. Clay was still outside retreating down the road until he was backed against the wall, his red coat a mark for every rifleman. His musket finally jamming, he caught up another, and, still firing, continued round to within sight of the gates, gaping wide. Through the smoke he saw more French, but making a run for it, stumbling over dead littering the entrance, he got inside in time to see 'Lt-Colonel Macdonell carrying a large piece of wood or the trunk of a tree ... One of his cheeks was marked with blood and his charger lay bleeding ...' Macdonell and a Sgt Graham got their shoulders to the gates while three officers firing from the gateway kept off more French until the new beam dropped in place. Stone slabs, more beams, were heaped. Above the brickwork hands, heads appeared as Frenchmen standing on each others' shoulders tried to climb over, before they were shot down. The yard became a killing ground: at last only one drummer boy was left alive.

From slopes behind, no one could make out much except that Hougoumont was hard pressed. Ensign Lake had an image of the Duke gazing 'intensely', of horse artillery 'coming up at a splitting pace', then his and three other companies of Coldstreamers were ordered down to retake the orchard as far as the woods. They lost it under renewed pressure, retook it again.

Some Coldstreamers reinforced the garden and yard through a side door; Clay was sent with one group to man the windows of an 'upper room of the château', commanding a field of fire over the tops of surrounding buildings. French guns were now between Hougoumont and the Allied ridge, pounding the main gates; again the entrance was stormed, letting a flood of assailants into the yard. A bayonet charge by last four Coldstream companies held in reserve cut them off while those inside were killed. Col. Woodford, although senior, agreed to serve under Macdonell, who knew the defences. Every window, loophole, the splintering gates themselves, were manned. Masonry chipped and crumbled under point blank gun fire but was too thick to be breached. Dense fog closed in over all-out siege.

Smoke had thickened above the garden and yard of Hougoumont for more than an hour, while the rest of the field waited. Lt Woodbury, nearly two miles away with 18th Hussars, on the far left flank, felt a 'silence of death'. Kincaid, from his advanced position by the sand pit, looked up from resetting the barricade to estimate finally some 10,000 infantry ranged in front, with more massed infantry and the gleam of armoured cavalry on each flank.

Across the valley by a rise in the road near Rosomme, Napoleon was seated at a table spread with maps. Although no orders had halted the mounting battle around Hougoumont, plans still specified a separate main assault on Wellington's centre, after a concentrated bombardment had first shattered his line. Amid the bustle of staff headquarters, the Emperor seemed 'depressed', his 'dull white complexion ... heavy walk ... very different from the General Bonaparte' that Col. Petiet, now a staff officer, had known in Italy.

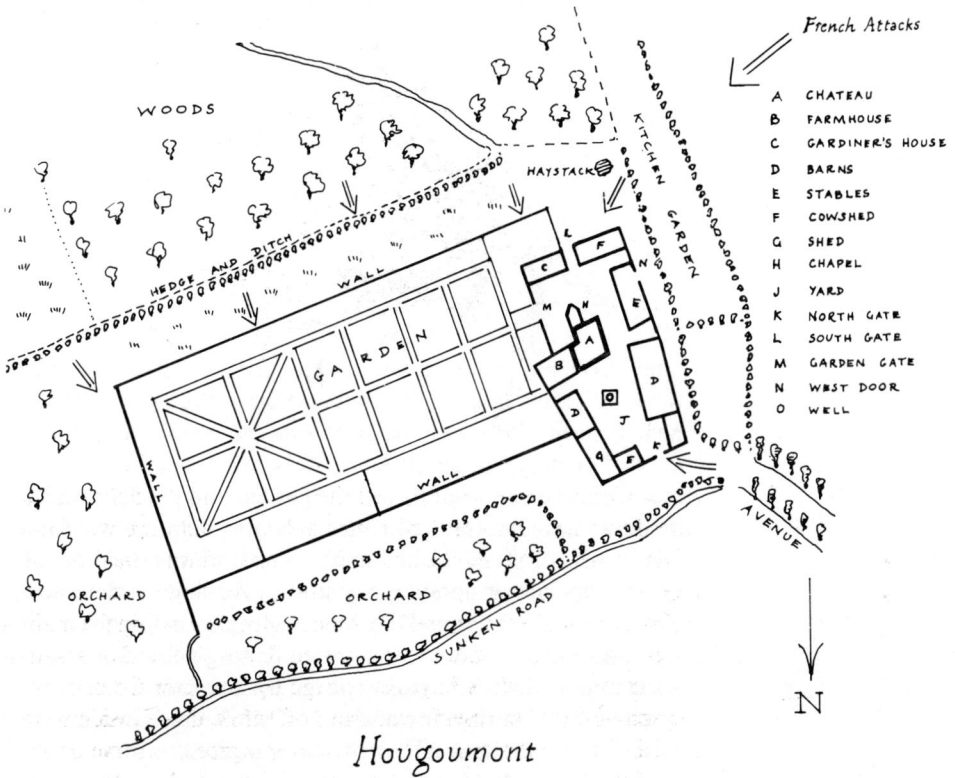

French Attacks

A   CHATEAU
B   FARMHOUSE
C   GARDINER'S HOUSE
D   BARNS
E   STABLES
F   COWSHED
G   SHED
H   CHAPEL
J   YARD
K   NORTH GATE
L   SOUTH GATE
M   GARDEN GATE
N   WEST DOOR
O   WELL

Hougoumont

About an hour ago Napoleon had been roused by reports of troops in the far eastern woods, and now a captured Prussian dispatch rider confirmed the worst: Bülow's advance guard was on the road. Against this threat two French cavalry divisions and two infantry were sent to the right as a flank protection. Directly ahead, however, more than a mile away, the colour of massed infantry and the glint of a vast array of artillery was at last confirmation that everything and everyone was in position, aligned, waiting.

At 1.30 p.m. a signal gun; then a shattering roar shook the ground: bombardment had begun.

14

$\mathscr{A}$ ROAR OF GUNS

One of the first shots landed on Kincaid's knoll, cutting clean through a tree, 'bringing down the whole of the bushy part', and nearly smothering two medical officers below. The French massed battery, all eighty guns, was firing steadily, two and three rounds per minute, in an inferno of sound. Even Peninsular men had heard nothing like this. Wheatley felt 'an undulation of the air'. First man killed in his battalion was only five files away, 'shrivelling up every muscle of the body', twirling his elbow 'round and round' in silent agony as he died. Cannon balls smashed wood or flesh literally to pieces. Black's unit lying under 'shells and balls a dozen for one minute'.

Waymouth, sitting down with 2nd Life Guards in a dip, saw ranks of Cumberland Hussars, still mounted, dropping when hit. Dalrymple's 15th Hussars had already had troops out

skirmishing with lancers on Nivelles road; now the regiment came under 'tremendous' cannonade. General Grant and staff crouched in the lee of a sunken road; nearby Verner's regiment dismounted and moved bodily into the road. As an ammunition wagon blew up they could 'distinctly hear the cheers of the enemy'. Verner noticed that horses got used to noise of cannon fire, 'but never to the whistling of bullets'. Gibney and other medical officers were already coping with first wounded, when they were ordered to make a new dressing station under cover, further back. Road to Mont St Jean now a death trap from fragments of chipped pave and ricocheting cannon balls bounding down its length, killing and rewounding many on the journey. Gibney no sooner arrived than he was recalled; all 15th now 'hugging the bank' against bombardment. Passing a canteen of gin, veterans astonished him by chatting casually about comrades killed, hiding their feelings as if they 'had only lost a finger'.

Mercer, unable to stand the suspense, was leading his troop up towards the front when a staff colonel angrily ordered him back to await orders. Dismounted and off the road again but with gun teams still in column, exposed now to shell-fire, Mercer wondered dismally if they were all to be killed without entering action at all.

Behind the battle for Hougoumont, Wellington ordered Mitchell's Brigade to replace Byng's. Light companies of 14th,

together with those of 51st, already lined a sunken road in the valley; now the remainder, ranged on slope behind, were sent forward. 'We marched in column of companies ... came upon an open valley ... the hill in front was fringed by the enemy's cannon ...' Keppel faced his first shellfire as the 14th formed square on an open plateau, a block to French lancers swarming around the Nivelles road, but an uncomfortable target for guns. A 51st skirmisher, mistaking the square for his own, ran in calling, 'Here I am, safe enough,' and instantly lost his head from a round shot. An ensign near Keppel, spattered with brains, raised a nervous laugh by drawling, 'How extremely disgusting.' A second shot swept away six bayonets; a third broke the chest of a sergeant; a freak shot killed 'the shortest man in the regiment, and in the very centre of the square'. 14th now ordered to lie, 'packed like herrings in a barrel'. Keppel squeezed on a drum with the colonel's horse pressed against his neck 'mumbling my epaulette, while I patted his cheek'.

Leaving Hougoumont secure for the moment, Wellington rode centre to main command post. His staff group, conspicuous on the skyline, had come under aimed fire; cannon shot was thudding repeatedly into the trunk of the elm. 'That's good practice ... I think they fire better here than in Spain,' observed the Duke coolly, but he sent back some of his party to shelter. British batteries, except those ranged on Hougoumont woods, were silent, gunners prone, reserving fire for the coming attack. Most troops withdrawn behind crest, lying or sitting in battle lines, some even sleeping. One exception was Bylandt's Belgian Brigade. Standing erect on forward slope, the Belgians were taking terrible casualties, their commanders perhaps thinking raw troops couldn't be trusted to move back without running.

Minutes dragged on: ten, twenty, thirty; remorselessly, steadily, methodically, French batteries smothered the crest. Without wind, a fog of smoke covered more than a mile of landscape. No one could see further than a few yards; no one could hear an order unless yelled in his ear.

15

*T*HE GREAT CHARGE

In lowest slopes, British light companies forming outer defence screen had been spared worst bombardment, but at 2 p.m. they came under a hail of musket fire. Through shredding smoke, half hidden by high corn, thousands of isolated tirailleurs were pressing forward, French guns firing over their heads.

92nd was in Allied 2nd line, half protected by the crest, except for shells coming in at high angle. The Regiment had been warned first attack would probably be by cavalry, and was now in column, sitting in ranks, each man with his arms, told to keep alert to obey any orders instantly – probably to form square. Men were being struck where they sat. Hope was with other officers when the Duke of Richmond brought a message, to be passed down the line: 'Blücher with 40,000' was coming up on Napoleon's right, and Wellington reckoned on 'complete victory'.

From his knoll, Kincaid could make out, beyond tirailleurs, huge columns on the move; heard now 'drums . . . the tantarara of trumpets . . . shouts . . . as if they had some hopes of scaring us off the ground . . .' Black could hardly believe his eyes: 'columns they were so thick . . . for two miles from Right to Left . . .' Royal Scots, like all Picton's front line, lying in double ranks, hedge in front. Only officers were on horseback.

Silence on Allied side at last broken by British batteries opening at full range, 1,500 yards. Behind their skirmishers, main French masses tramped slowly nearer. Frequent bursts of white smoke left gaps of fallen; ranks closed up automatically. The chant of *'Vive l'Empereur!'* came in waves. All British guns were firing shell or round shot, but canister lay ready.

In the valley, Count d'Erlon's French Corps had four divisions, 20,000 men in all, marching in four columns staggered left in front; each column formed by battalions in line, three ranks deep, five or six paces between battalions, four and five battalions to a brigade, two brigades making each divisional mass 180 men wide, about 30 deep. Extended depth gave solidity and weight; fairly wide frontage made deployment easier if needed. Skirmishers were still in front, a division of Reille's on the left, cavalry on flanks, and behind all, an addition only the French possessed: mobile ambulances. Baron Larrey, famous Surgeon-in-Chief of Napoleon's armies, world authority on war wounds, rode beside assistants and the light two-wheel carts with sliding stretchers he had designed.

To Wellington, such a massive attack, plus reserves which must be hidden in rear, meant the bulk of Napoleon's army was almost certainly deployed against him. No hope of holding such numbers for long; everything depended on Blücher. Although his face might not have shown it, impatience for firm news became suddenly acute. He sent off Muffling to the left to make first contact, to co-ordinate the Prussians' arrival and thereafter to take overall command of the left wing. This would go some way towards surmounting the inexperience of the Prince of Orange, still officially 1st Corps commander.

First assailed point was the advanced bastion of La Haye Sainte. Baring's outlying riflemen were driven by heavy fire through the south orchard; a Lüneburg battalion was sent as reinforcements; the Germans retook the orchard only to find cuirassiers in front and infantry surrounding the garden to rear. Baring ordered all defenders back into the buildings.

Everywhere in the centre, clouds of skirmishers were forging ahead. Kincaid's riflemen on the knoll were firing steadily and accurately, but French swept by on both sides and to avoid being cut off the 95th's companies retreated. Drums, shouts rose from the massed columns advancing close behind skirmishers; beside and behind them the helmeted cavalry.

Mercer, at long last with orders, had galloped up to high ground behind Hougoumont and unlimbered facing right, across a ravine, near Keppel's 3/14th. Beyond Mercer 'the corn ... was full of French riflemen'; Germans, half hidden in corn his side, were firing back. Mercer's brief was to watch the Nivelles road. Shot from a French battery to his left was falling short, but howitzer shells 'spitting and spluttering' soon had his range. Looking back and left he was alarmed to see 'shoals of lancers' like 'a heavy surf breaking' sweep up the main slope. More shells were bursting by his guns; finally he disobeyed standing orders by replying. Immediately an answer from six heavy 12 pdrs; the last shot of their salvo shattered a gunner's arm to pieces. Mercer would 'never forget the scream ...' Watching officers from other units were running, one medico on hands and knees 'still holding his umbrella up' scrambling away 'like a great baboon', convulsing gun teams with laughter.

No one laughing in the centre. Kincaid, his men running for

safety, had just time to dash his horse through a hedge gap when he saw 95th reserves also falling back, under mistaken orders. Shouting and waving desperately, he managed to halt them ten yards from the hedge, and held a three company line there until remainder of their brigade, under General Kempt, advanced from rear to their support. Accurate rifle fire was cutting down

French by scores, but led by officers 'dancing and flourishing their swords' they gained a foothold on the knoll and began fanning out in line up to the hedge. To the left other French columns were tramping steadily uphill through mud, men cheering hoarsely. French batteries ceased as they neared the crest, but British gunners tore their ranks with canister down to fifty yards, before themselves dashing for cover.

Wellington had crossed the main road east towards the new danger point. Jackson, just ridden in from Brussels, found all except one A.D.C. sheltering behind the crest. Dismounting himself and looking over his own saddle he could 'just trace the outlines of the Duke and his horse amidst the smoke, standing very near the Highlanders ...'

Picton, divisional commander, was well up facing the storm. Through the roar of musketry someone shouted to him that Bylandt's Brigade, barely visible, looked about to give way. 'Never mind, they shall have a taste of it,' he growled. The Belgians, already hopelessly shattered and demoralized, let off a few ragged shots before the whole brigade took to its heels.

All Picton's V Division was still lying down, below line of sight over the crest. To front ranks of wildly cheering French it seemed the position was swept bare, guns deserted, victory in sight.

Then, under shouted commands, Kempt's Brigade was on its feet and Picton was leading 28th and 32nd, Gloucester and Cornwall regiments, towards the gap. They crashed through the hedge, formed up on flank of the French column, fired one volley, and under colours streaming advanced with fixed bayonets. Two regiments from Pack's Brigade, Royal Scots and 2/44th East Essex, moved on the eastern flank and poured in close fire, but were gradually forced back by weight of numbers. Pressure almost irresistible: near the centre road, Col. Douglas's thin line of 79th, Camerons, was crumbling. Picton was riding through; even in the din Capt. Seymour, a cavalry staff officer, heard his tremendous shout to 'Rally the Highlanders!' – then he felt his horse fall and at the same moment saw Picton drop. He reached the body in time to prevent a soldier taking a purse, but Wellington's best general lay dead, to be carried back by two grenadiers of the 32nd. The plain round hat had a bullet hole above the brim.

Kempt, taking over from Picton, was galloping along the line trying to stem disaster, calling to Kincaid 'never to quit that spot'. Kincaid had time to realize cuirassiers were coming straight towards him, found to his horror his sword had rusted and was stuck in its scabbard; then, standing helpless, saw the pattern change before his eyes.

Survivors of the 92nd, 300 or so men, were still lying in reserve, unable to see the crest for smoke, when Lt Winchester heard Pack galloping up, crying '92nd, everything has given way on your right and left and you must charge ...' On their feet now, drums beating, bayonets fixed, they walked forward. French had halted by the hedge, apparently reforming and reloading, when through the murk the small but disciplined formation loomed like apparitions, a mere twenty yards away. At point blank range, 92nd fired a double volley, front ranks then rear, then went into a screaming charge.

Uxbridge had seen from Wellington's command post the threatened break through and was riding back to alert British heavy cavalry. Somerset's Household Brigade, 1,200 strong, was already in line: 1st Life Guards on right, King's Dragoon Guards centre, 2nd Life Guards left, with Blues or Royal Horse Guards in rear as supports. While Uxbridge crossed the fields to warn Union Brigade some 600 yards east, Household troops began the advance to the summit, battle uproar keeping each man watching for hand signals. No verbal orders possible.

Union Brigade was moving now, under renewed French shelling. Capt. Phipps of 1st Royals managed to hear Uxbridge's 'The Royals and Inniskillings will charge, the Greys support', before he galloped away. Major Evans, acting as A.D.C., went forward with General Ponsonby to judge the 'proper time for the Brigade to come up'; both stood waiting amid the inferno. Behind and to the right, Household Brigade heard bugles; Capt. Elton in 1st Dragoon Guards suddenly found the walk had become a trot; 'without waiting for any particular order drew swords ...' 1st Life Guards were pacing his right, but 2nd Life Guards 'still moving by threes', left squadron trailing, trying to 'scramble into line' as best it could. Advance quickened. Uxbridge, in front, was over the crest, crossing ground 'dreadfully broken' by shell bursts, descending forward slope. Ahead, Elton saw Allied infantry curling back 'into solid squares', beyond them 'the crests of the cuirassiers'.

Further left, Union Brigade was taking more casualties: Col. Miller's Inniskillings 'dismounted and marched up ... on foot', remounting near crest. Corporal Dickson, in 2nd rank of Greys, glimpsed the bonnets of Highlanders and the flash of bayonets beyond a holly hedge. Strictly, supporting cavalry should not join a main charge, but officers as well as men were at fever pitch. Dickson saw Ponsonby turn as if to signal, saw the general's horse suddenly rear and his cloak fall, Ponsonby

stooping, and then Evans waving his hat. His colonel was mouthing the order 'Scots Greys, charge!', then 'waving his sword' was riding 'straight at the hedges . . . a great cheer rose from our ranks . . .' To the right, Miller's Inniskillings heard a man in plain clothes – the Duke of Richmond – yelling 'Now's your time'; Dickson felt his charger take the hedge 'at terrific speed'; troopers were wildly urging horses down and up the steep slippery banks of the road; on far side trumpeters sounding charge even before line reformed. Lt Wyndham, in the Greys, noticed the ring of bullets on swords, 'no order of parade . . . pêle-mêle we went . . .' As the 400 Scottish troopers saw kilted infantry in front a tremendous roar went up: 'Hurrah, 92nd! Scotland for ever!' Through all the din the skirl of pipes; Dickson 'plainly saw my old friend Pipe-Major Cameron standing apart on a hillock coolly playing "Hey Johnny Cope, are ye waulkin' yet?" . . . Our colonel went on before us, past our guns and down the slope . . .' Young Armour 'our rough-rider from Mauchline' riding in front of Dickson. British infantry was trying to wheel back by sections but 'some of them had not time to get clear . . . one young lad crying out, "Eh! but I dinna think ye wad ha'e hurt me sae."' Dragoons passing feathered Highland bonnets now, long-suffering Gordons delirious: 'Go at them, the Greys!' 'Many of the Highlanders grasped our stirrups . . . and dashed with us into the fight.' Gathering momentum, heavy swords held straight out, lines of Dragoons crashed into helpless French infantry. Behind them, the bayonets of 92nd. Hope 'never saw . . . the regiment so very savage . . . they repeatedly cried to the cavalry to spare none . . .' Troopers 'lopping off heads at every stroke'. French, caught while deploying, couldn't move, lying on ground crying to 92nd to save them from 'those dragoons'. One poor fellow offered Robertson 'his watch and all his money' but the line swept on. All Pack's regiments joined the carnage: Anton, in 42nd, saw 'swords streaming in blood, waving . . . descending . . . like the turning of a flail . . .'

Across Genappe road, Household Brigade well into charge, cuirassiers ahead. Waymouth on its left: 'Ponsonby's Heavy Brigade also charging with us, in a nearly parallel line . . .' As pace increased to a gallop, Major Kelly in the Life Guards on extreme right saw left of line and cuirassiers 'come to the shock like two walls'. Bigger men on fresh, bigger horses, forcing sideways, were driving French back. Behind Household troops Whinyates had all thirteen rocket sections following: one section used remains of abattis as a platform before firing through the corn.

Smell of sweat and powder, blinding smoke and sudden

movement after hours of waiting induced a kind of frenzy. One man, Dakin, seen 'foaming at the mouth'. Shaw, fighting two cuirassiers at once, cleaved right through a helmet, the face falling off 'like a bit of apple'. Armour no protection: Life Guards cutting reins, slashing at legs, finally thrusting 'under the arm, and in the groin'. Chapman: 'the most dreadful slaughter . . . they run like a hare before the hounds . . .' Beyond La Haye Sainte, scores of cuirassiers were toppled bodily down a steep road cutting.

All d'Erlon's columns halted, trapped on flank, blocked in front. Kennedy, riding with 1st Royals, led a savage charge on a French colour party and captured the eagle of 105th regiment. Near Dickson, away on left, a huge Greys sergeant, Charles Ewart, was 'slashing right and left' at five or six of another colour party. Killing two, he cut down bearer and grabbed the eagle, was attacked desperately in his turn; parrying bayonet and lance he slashed three more men through head and teeth, one 'from the chin upwards'.

French formations suddenly crumbling, rear ranks fleeing. Panic seized helpless men so packed they could not use their muskets. Thousands of prisoners were left unguarded in the wild advance. Kincaid, staring from the crossroads: 'hundreds . . . threw themselves down, and pretended to be dead, while the cavalry galloped over them . . . I never saw such a scene in my life.'

British infantry, under strict orders not to leave their position, were returning uphill leaving heavy cavalry alone in valley bottom. Buglers sounding 'Rally' in vain; no one, not even officers, in any mood to listen. Close ahead now the hated guns. Dickson heard his colonel: 'Charge! Charge the guns!' Col. Hamilton was later seen with hands cut off, riding with stirrups, reins in his mouth. 'Then we ... sabred the gunners, lamed the horses, and cut their traces ... The artillery drivers ... weeping aloud ... mere boys ...' Dickson's horse actually biting and tearing with its teeth before it sank. He sprang on to another saddle, rode on towards the heart of the French position. But frothing horses were tiring fast.

Southwards, an impassive, squat figure was watching, from a new advanced command post formed at La Belle Alliance. Half admiring, half astonished at British audacity, Napoleon ordered up waiting lancers.

British cavalry was riding in scattered groups, squadrons mixed, all formation lost. With about twenty others – Royals, Inniskillings, Greys – without officers, Dickson saw lancers cutting off their rear. Shouting 'Come on, lads; that's the road home!' they steered head on. Dickson saw 'lancers rise and fall ... the leading man of ours go down ...' Dragoons were warding off lances with bare hands; French viciously spearing, respearing men as they lay. In sucking mud, Union horses could 'hardly drag their feet'. Jumping clear, Dickson passed Brigade commander Ponsonby dead beside his bay, his coat blown aside, a 'miniature of a lady and his watch' by his hand.

All through the valley, troopers were paying the price of their mad charge. Shaw, riding beside Capt. Kelly, was last seen surrounded, sword broken in his hand, fighting with his helmet before he vanished under his assailants. Waymouth, already

wounded, was saved by Surgeon Larrey, whose ambulances had been almost overrun in the charge. He knocked aside a French musket and, kneeling, spoke some broken English; showed him a penknife bought in London.

One trooper, a 6-ft 4-inch giant whom the artist Haydon knew, had never used his sword before: his first stroke against a cuirass nearly broke his arm. As he cut at a horse's neck, the rider's helmet fell, showing 'a bald head and white hairs'; but startled by more lancers he cleaved it in two and escaped. The image of white hairs troubled him for the rest of his life.

Victorious lancers were now within striking distance of the Allied line. Uxbridge had given all his cavalry commanders permission to act on their own initiative 'within limits'; and now Vandeleur, to save remnants of heavy cavalry from complete destruction, ordered his brigade into the charge. Like Union Brigade before them, Light Dragoons couldn't stop: driving their way through hand-to-hand fighting they rode as far as the French battery. But other French guns were firing; lancers, at first scattered, now regathered and counter-charged with cuirassiers; and dragoons retreated.

Hay's course took him right across the valley to above Hougoumont, into lines of 71st, when stopping 'to see the last man down the sloping . . . banks' a shell burst under his horse. Sliding over its tail, he was trying to kick the animal up when a warning shout alerted him to two lancers coming full tilt. He jumped the bank just as musket fire brought them down.

Fresh cavalry were everywhere; French guns firing harder than ever as survivors of heavy brigades trailed back through extreme flank. Vivian, 'exposed to the most dreadful fire', made limited charges to cover their retreat.

Mercer was in the thick of another storm, from French batteries shooting clear of cuirassiers. He could see men dropping in Bolton's troop to his left, Bolton himself killed. Behind the nearest gun, drivers unharnessed one of the horses and repeatedly drove it away, finally leading it right back to the rear. Minutes later, Mercer heard a shout, and turned to find the panting beast close beside one of his ammunition teams, the driver waving in horror: it was still living, with half a head, nothing below the eyes.

Gunfire shutting out all other sound. Against general smoke 'still more dense columns . . . rising straight into the air like a giant pillar . . . the explosions of ammunition waggons . . .' Seen, but silent. Dimly Mercer could make out sweeping cavalry, charge and counter-charge passing through each other like 'the fingers of the right hand through those of the left'. One advance nearly reached his battery. A colonel thought the situation 'desperate', with only one retreat road certain disaster. Mercer could only 'trust in the Duke' to 'get us out of it somehow'. But lest the guns had to be abandoned, he ordered numbers one to have spikes ready to hammer into vent holes, so as to make firing impossible.

At last, almost suddenly, the lancers were gone. Up on the crest Uxbridge rode in. Some officers congratulated him on his tremendous charge, on the overthrow of a complete infantry corps; but he knew his own heavy brigades of the finest cavalry were almost destroyed. 1,200 men, many of them wounded, had returned out of 2,000; 1,000 horses lost. The army no longer had a heavy assault arm.

$\mathscr{C}$UIRASSIERS AND SQUARES

Four and a half miles westward, at Chapelle St Lambert, Bülow's corps was reassembling after a two-hour halt. The weary columns, slithering through deep lanes, sandwiched between guns and wagons and delayed by a fire which blocked the road at Wavre, urged on unceasingly by Blücher, had begun arriving at noon – just half way. Gneisenau argued long with Blücher about the danger of crossing the Lasne and threading the tangled forest ahead; but as gunfire from Waterloo boomed and muttered, advance guard finally set off again at 2.30 p.m.

Gneisenau needn't have worried. Grouchy was miles south, refusing to change his route even when his staff also detected the murmur of guns. His orders specified Wavre, and as the last

of two whole Prussian corps cleared the town, Grouchy's corps was still marching towards it.

Near Hougoumont, Frazer was holding his watch: exactly at 2.45 he saw plumes of black dense smoke rising from the barns and outhouses. Exploding howitzer shells had set straw and woodwork alight; soon the fire reached the château, where Clay and others lined the windows of an upper room. Their officer barred the doorway, keeping men choking at their post until the floor began to collapse, several of them 'more or less injured' struggling out through the embers. In the yard horses bolted from the flaming barn, circled in terror and rushed back in; Standen watched helplessly, astonished that they remained there to be burnt. Chilling screams came from a stable, but flames were too fierce to reach the wounded, French and English, laid inside. Rolling smoke spurred French artillery to redoubled efforts. North carriage gates were again blasted loose, again blocked; solid shot pounded the walls; Clay's party were sent running to man a breach over the southern entrance where 'shattered fragments of the wall were mixed up with the bodies of our dead . . .' Clay took one side, Sgt Aston the other.

As the inferno raged, Wellington sent down a pencilled order to Macdonell: '. . . keep your men in those parts to which the fire does not reach. Take care that no men are lost by the falling in of the roof or floors . . . occupy the ruined walls inside of the garden . . .'

More troops swelled the French attacks, from two divisions; from Allied line nine companies of Byng's 2/3rd Guards and a whole battalion of the German Legion joined the defenders: dead and wounded piled in garden, orchard, along the blackened walls.

Elsewhere the field was clear except for skirmishers again pushed out by each side, and artillery. With teams reinforced or replaced, every available French gun was firing, raising bombardment to new intensity.

Kempt's Brigade had moved to fill the gap left by Bylandt's; and Wellington ordered veterans of Lambert's Brigade to new reserve position behind far left. Lawrence was marching with 40th 'up to action in open column' when a shell cut through two men and exploded at his feet, hurling him 'at least two yards in the air', but leaving him only grazed and shaken. One recruit fell to the ground, paralysed by fear. Lawrence was contemptuous: 'it's the smell of this little powder that has caused your illness . . .', but neither words nor kicks could shift the man and he was left lying.

Ahead, all Allied infantry were back over crest, crouching in what shelter they could find.

Marshal Ney, Napoleon's battle commander, had seen two infantry attacks fail. Now, through the swirling smoke it seemed the red lines of British defences were retreating, leaving crest wide open for a third, swift assault before they could reform.

With d'Erlon's Corps broken and Reille's bogged down around Hougoumont, it would have to be by cavalry. Only half of the army's 20,000 magnificent horsemen were with Grouchy or in reserve: hardly any of remainder had yet been used. As couriers rode with orders, General Milhaud's 2,700 cuirassiers, lancers from the *Garde*, lastly chasseurs, formed three massive lines, 5,100 strong. Ney himself led the advance.

From the ridge Wellington and Allied officers, gazing through glasses at the distant glitter of helmets and pennants, could hardly believe their eyes. Amazingly, French cavalry, apparently without support, was advancing against intact infantry and guns still in position.

Orders went to all front line infantry to prepare to form square; General Alten's division actually oblongs. Every man knew it was vital to be ready: the 69th had been almost wiped out two days ago when caught in line at Quatre Bras.

Already, three quarters of a mile away, enemy cavalry was separating into squadrons, beginning to bunch in staggered formation, funnelled towards the 1,000 yard gap between La Haye Sainte and Hougoumont. From nearest defended corner of each, musket fire further limited open front to about 600 yards: Ney's huge mass couldn't strike simultaneously anyway. Soldiers, crouching on the ground, could see now without telescopes the formidable sight growing clearer every minute. To Gronow, with Maitland's Guards, 'an overwhelming ... line ... ever advancing ... glittered like a strong wave of the sea'. British and Hanoverian batteries, drowning the thunder of hooves, were firing solid shot at full range, under orders to run for shelter at the last moment.

High corn and greasy mud were tiring horses but hardly slowed their last steady trot uphill. Amid a storm of shot, French spurred to a final effort and then they were past the guns. Ahead lay only the small red squares. Mercer, through the smoke: 'a dark mass of cavalry appeared for an instant on the main ridge, and then came sweeping down the slope in swarms ...' so numerous that infantry appeared completely submerged. But horses refused all attempts to charge massed bayonets and simply carried their riders between squares, to be exposed to murderous company volleys from each side. 'Crossing, turning, riding ... apparently without any object', many were making for Mercer's guns. Gould muttered, 'I fear all is over.' The 3/14th stood in square while Mercer's men struggled to drag trails to face guns left, on new targets – then all at once the first wave of cavalry was gone, dispersing down the valley.

Retreat brought no rest, however: French guns, briefly silent when masked by last stage of Ney's advance, re-opened unending bombardment. Mercer again: Frazer 'galloped up, crying out, "Left limber up, and as fast as you can."' Face 'as black as a chimney sweep's', one sleeve torn, Frazer bellowed his orders as they rode, guns bouncing behind them. More attacks were coming; if French persisted in 'charging home, you do not expose your men, but retire ... into the adjacent square ...'

Up the reverse slope of the crest they met 'a new atmosphere ... suffocatingly hot'. Smoke hid everything but through roar of guns they could 'distinctly hear ... a mysterious humming noise, like ... myriads of black beetles' from a hail of bullets 'so

thick ... it seemed dangerous to extend the arm ...' The surgeon, new to action, couldn't make it out, 'My God, Mercer, what *is* that?' A cannon shot hissed past. '*There! – there!* What *is* it all?' Mercer persuaded him to move to rear before his troop went into position between two squares of Brunswickers 'falling fast ... making great gaps in their squares ... officers and sergeants ... pushing their men together, and sometimes

thumping them ... like so many logs', utterly dazed by gunfire. Mercer thought it madness to retire on such 'supports'; they would probably fly the moment his gunners moved.

Skirmish line was again pushing down forward slope. With all other officers killed, seventeen-year-old Macready now commanded his light company, standing under 'a hurricane of small shot' when a runner from Halkett brought orders to come in. 'As our bugler was killed I shouted and made signals to move by the left ...' One third of the company was left lying in the corn, dead or dying. Returning, he paused by Lloyd's abandoned battery, and took in a scene 'grand beyond description. Hougoumont and its wood sent up a broad flame through the dark masses of smoke ...' French cavalry dimly visible as 'a waving mass of long red feathers', elsewhere 'gleams as from a sheet of steel showed that the cuirassiers were moving ... cannon were belching forth fire ...': all together like one 'labouring volcano'.

Ahead, Macready's regiment and 73rd had combined in one square, 33rd and 69th in another. He had hardly rejoined before shouts warned of a new charge. Horsemen were forming only

100 yards away; again the heavy trot uphill began to quicken to a gallop. Macready had a terrifying glimpse of heads bent 'so that the peak of their helmets looked like visors', of gigantic figures that seemed 'cased in armour from the plume to the saddle'. In a King's Legion square to the left, Wheatley's heart failed at the flash of iron; rumours had spread through the whole army last week that muskets were useless against cuirassiers' armour. Shouts of 'Stand firm!' 'Stand fast!' and then 'sabres in the air ... sun gleaming on the steel', horsehair streaming from crests, towering horsemen were on them.

Mercer's guns were still going into position when warning cries came from nearby squares, and leading squadrons burst through the smoke within 100 yards. He ordered case, and gunners began methodically loading, ramming, inserting vent quills, standing with slow match. On 'Fire!', the first round of packed lethal balls slowed front rank to a walk; then whole salvo took terrible effect, piling the ground with men and horses; 'Still they persevered ... though slowly ...'

Squares let cavalry come even closer, Macready's to within thirty yards before the first volley brought 'helmets falling – cavaliers starting from their seats with convulsive springs ... horses plunging ...' Along three-quarters of a mile of ridge, dozens of squares delivering controlled, company volleys; rear two ranks of every face firing, while front two knelt, muskets remaining loaded, bayonets hedged against pounding hooves. Like a tide, packed cuirassiers advanced over their fallen, those in front forced ever forward by weight of numbers behind.

Most gun teams had run for shelter, but Mercer's were blasting oncoming lines over a raised roadside, at point blank range. Every discharge brought down more, but others pressed behind. A spongeman slipped and fell across a muzzle, 'both his arms ... blown off at the elbows', looking up 'piteously'. Just as all seemed lost, riders began turning to each side trying to escape; some galloped on singly past Mercer's guns, the rest 'a complete mob ... actually ... using the pommels of their swords to fight their way out' through their own ranks, while his six guns cut swathes. Then rear ranks wheeled about, and with at last space to move the whole body was streaming away downhill.

Everywhere the attack was broken; squares were standing. One party of 100 cuirassiers, passing right through the line and trying to reach safety back along the Nivelles road, galloped into an ambushed road block lined by Wheeler's company. Only 'one solitary individual' escaped.

As the wave retreated, light companies again descended the fields, and gunners returned to guns. None had been spiked: Jackson saw Lloyd reach one of his left loaded before his team, and fired it single-handed. French batteries were roaring. No one believed attacks were finished; now Wellington brought up Adam's Brigade to forward slopes by north-east corner of Hougoumont. Leeke passed ground strewn with remains left by a Brunswick square after it moved; one soldier, leg torn off and face black from explosion, caught 'hold of the hand of one of our men' before dying. Some 200 yards in front of British batteries, Adam's four regiments formed two strong squares, able to cut into flanks of new cavalry attacks, but forced to stand or lie under artillery fire for next two and a half hours. Soldier Tom 'lay on the face of a brae', so tired actually dozing when the young boy beside him lost both legs, 'cut very close'. He begged Tom not to tell his mother how he died: 'If she saw me thus, it would break her heart; farewell ...'

Infantry, unable to move out of square for fear of cavalry – already reforming – were now exposed to constant cannonade. Wheatley saw 'a cannon ball take away a Colonel of the Nassau Regiment so cleanly that the horse never moved ...' Morris, crouching in 2nd rank of 73rd, enduring deafening volleys fired over his head, saw the next square temporarily broken; Wellington, speaking with Halkett, rode into his for refuge. Again oncoming cavalry divided, forced between staggered squares. A Guards officer watched 'cross fire cut them to pieces, our men standing like statues ...' The slope in front of Hope's 92nd was 'completely covered with the mangled corpses', wounded lying among them in constant terror of being 'trod to death by their horses'. Mercifully, cries of the dying almost unheard through the uproar, but the chant from thousands of throats of *'Vive l'Empereur!'* rose like the murmuring of a 'bee-hive'.

Despite courage 'bordering on frenzy' another attack faltered. Wheatley saw Wellington leave Morris's square and gallop for the Life Guards waving his hat; weakened British squadrons were at least able to drive French survivors down the slope. But used non-stop, musket ammunition was beginning to run low. An artillery wagon lurched up to Macready's square, emptying '2 or 3 casks of cartridges'.

Through the smoke pall, in front of invisible cavalry, French skirmishers were again pressing forward. Mercer's gunners 'obliged to stand with port-fires lighted', under musket and pistol fire from forty yards. Trusting to poor marksmanship, Mercer encouraged his men by 'a promenade ... up and down our front'; after a near miss he taunted and shook his finger. 'The rogue grinned as he reloaded', but after 'a terrible time' in aiming missed again.

In the valley, Ney simply could not believe the British position could withstand one last attack. Once more lines of cuirassiers struggled uphill, slipping, plunging, stepping over wounded. Skirmishers in front of Mercer wheeled away to let a new wall of men advance at 'slow but steady trot' – silent but for the rumble of hooves, led by an officer with 'breast covered with decorations'. Guns, double loaded, round shot behind case, opened at fifty yards, bringing again the awful carnage; the ground became almost impassable for fallen.

Even in battered squares morale was rising. If only they could keep formation, men realized they were safe. Macready heard a contemptuous growl: 'Here come these damned fools again.' Under savage artillery fire between attacks, squares were shrinking, though: Gronow's 'at 4 o'clock ... a perfect hospital', in which it was impossible not to tread on dead or wounded. Men were suffocating in powder fumes, blackened, mouths gritted. Wheatley firing a wounded soldier's musket until his shoulder 'nearly jellied'.

Elderly Sir George Wood, commanding artillery, appeared at Mercer's battery, 'blinking as a man does when facing a gale of wind'. 'Damn it ... you have hot work of it here.' Attack followed attack; no one counted their exact number. But 'shaking and covered with foam', exhausted horses, walking now, refused all spurring towards the bristling bayonets; frantic horsemen could only brandish their swords helplessly until shot down. Half poisoned and blinded, walled in by choking smoke, squares were never broken; time and again infantry withstood cavalry.

Seeing the French tiring, sure now Prussians must be very near, even Wellington showed his excitement: 'By God, Adam, I think we shall beat them yet!'

Simmons, continually leading sorties by 95th against skirmishers, was cheering a friend, Lt Felix, who with a cap and

jacket ripped by bullets was sure he would be killed. 'Nonsense
... the Devil a feather will they touch me,' he laughed, when he
felt the smashing impact of a bullet through his ribs, which
broke his watch and left the hands at 4 p.m. He was carried back
to Mont St Jean farm cowhouse, where the ground was thick
with wounded and dying. Verner, walking back with a head
wound, found shelling there worse than at the front, shot
and shell plunging the length of the road.

Servicing guns was becoming more difficult. Overheated
barrels slowed rate of fire, for fear of premature explosions;
vent holes enlarged dangerously; run up after recoil was by
hand, and without horses some guns were driven further and
further out of position. French cavalry were reduced to
isolated, forlorn attempts to break the deadlock. Morris had to
face a cuirassier who somehow 'deliberately walked his horse
up to the bayonet's point'; he shut his eyes as the Frenchman
leaned over to thrust with his sword – only to find the man shot
down. Macready saw the Frenchman dragged inside the
square, 'his only cry ... "*tirez donc, tirez – tirez ...* "'. Mad with
pain or rage the wounded man thrust a bayonet into his neck,
then 'raised up his cuirass plunged it into his stomach and kept
working it about till he ceased to breathe'.

Everywhere stalemate: Jackson was astonished to see prowl-
ing cuirassiers vainly watching for an opening, unable to
charge, while infantry refused to fire and leave themselves
unloaded. As Wellington, looking 'thoughtful and pale', sheltered for some minutes in Gronow's square, exasperated
guardsmen, tried beyond endurance, began shouting for British
cavalry; 'Why don't they come and pitch in to those French ...'
16th and 23rd Light Dragoons did charge, 'cheered' as they
passed Macready's square, but were soon forced back. Some
Belgian cavalry had halted; Halkett rode up to lead them on,
then the plumed Prince of Orange; but the Belgians scattered
from bursting shells. This time French cavalry retreated only to
their gun line; some pieces were brought to within 150 yards,
firing grape and horsenails 'making complete lanes through

us'. Morris's square 'throwing the dead outside', pulling the wounded in. Two men fell beside him. A shell burned down its fuse while ranks stood, unable to move, and exploded to kill or maim seventeen, lodging a splinter in his cheek. 'Our situation now was truly awful ... Our poor old Captain was horribly frightened, and several times came to me for a drop of something to keep his spirits up.' He was later cut in two by a cannon shot.

Leeke, behind front face of 52nd, realized he could sometimes follow projectiles winging overhead from British guns, but almost never those from the enemy. A gleam of sun suddenly revealed a French team sponging out their piece, alarmingly near. He saw the flash, the glint of the ball in a direct line. Gathering all his strength he stood gripping his colour staff for an eternity of two whole seconds before the shot smashed through four men, missed his pole by inches, and bounded out over the rear face of the square. In the bloody, shrinking centres, terrible disfigurements. One colonel saw a man's leg, broken through the knee, swell above it to 'the size of his body'.

But three hours of torment could not destroy the discipline which held men together. 'Before the action began Col. Ellis had ordered all officers of his regiment, 23rd Royal Welch Fusiliers, to see that no man left his post to attend any wounded, whoever it should be, including himself. Now, shot in the side, the colonel 'quietly left the square alone, and was seen to fall from his horse soon after', and was left to die. Morris heard his Sgt-Major, 'turned deadly pale', tell his colonel, 'We had nothing like this in Spain, Sir.' He was killed minutes later. Wellington, riding when he could from regiment to regiment, bearing a charmed life, encouraged the officers of one: 'Hard pounding this, gentlemen, let's see who will pound longest.'

At last came a lull; with no wind the smoke took time to clear; then from Lambert's Brigade Harry Smith saw 'the scanty lines of red in their old position, and a cheer along the whole line ...'

17

A CLOUD OF SKIRMISHERS

It was now 5.30 p.m., three and a half hours since the first massive infantry assault under d'Erlon had set out to clear the crest; and despite all efforts not one part of Wellington's position had fallen. Since 4 p.m. men from Bülow's Corps had been filtering out from Paris Wood along the Lasne road; in the last half hour Prussians in fierce fighting had driven Lobau's lines back into Plancenoit, and were within a mile of encircling the whole French army.

Napoleon, for the first time, faced stark defeat. He ordered east a division of Young Guard from his last reserve; but although they threw back the Prussians from Plancenoit, time was ebbing fast. An all-out attack by infantry was directed to take La Haye Sainte, at any cost, to allow guns to be planted on the knoll above it and blast the crest at point blank range.

Minutes later, forward Allied officers like Black of the 3/1st faced the extraordinary advance, 'about 10,000 skirmishers you never saw such a sight . . . all dispersed . . .' As they surrounded La Haye Sainte, the end was near. Major Baring had sent repeated requests, but wagons of special rifle cartridges had been either lost or blown up. The garrison's sixty rounds per man were almost finished; even Nassau troops with muskets had nothing, relief parties cut off. Attackers swarmed against walls, loopholes; there were seventeen dead piled by the open entrance to the barn. It caught fire; Nassauers relayed water by camp kettle. As Baring sent a last message that he could hold no longer the French, realizing defenders could not fire back, began shooting them down from roof and walls. Another barn door was forced; the passage beyond blocked with bayonets.

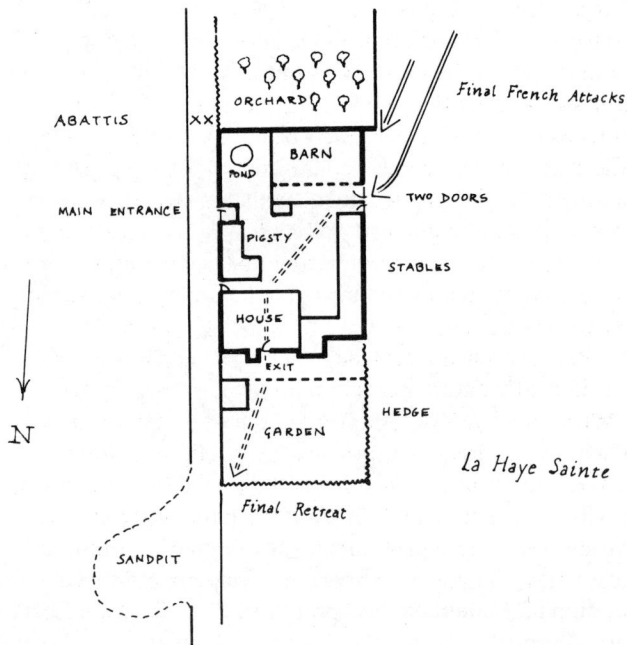

Seeing the farm surrounded, the Prince of Orange ordered Ompteda's King's German Legion Brigade, standing in square, to form line and advance. Ompteda, an experienced professional, argued that lurking cuirassiers made such a move suicide – at the least he needed cavalry support. The Prince refused to listen: 'I must still repeat my order to attack in line with the bayonet . . .' At last Ompteda drew his sword. 'Try and save my two nephews,' he called to one of his colonels, then led the remains of 5th and 8th Line regiments, 200 men, into murderous musket fire. Wheatley, walking forward with 5th Line, at sixty yards from the enemy heard bugles and shouted 'Charge!' Beside men 'huzzaing' wildly he ran at a drummer and was lifting his sword when he fell senseless.

French cavalry, seizing their chance, had cut in on flank, almost annihilating 8th Regiment and part of 5th, which just managed to form square. One officer saw the solitary figure of Ompteda, conspicuous with white plume of rank, ride calmly right up to the enemy line; saw French officers, as if amazed, knock aside their men's muskets; then the sword strokes of the horseman 'smite the shakos off'; then saw Ompteda in the enemy's midst 'sink from his horse and vanish'.

Inside the farm, an eighteen-year-old Scottish lieutenant, George Graeme, headed a last hand-to-hand defence behind the smashed door. He tried to 'halt the men and make one more charge' down the passage, but French marksmen simply cut them down. A Frenchman aimed at Graeme; a German stabbed the attacker 'in the mouth and out through his neck'; a sudden rush swept defenders back into the house, behind furniture, under beds; infuriated French began shooting wounded. One officer grabbed Graeme's collar and waved up four men with bayonets but he parried them with his sword. Realizing the French looked 'frightened and pale as ashes', he thought 'you shan't keep me', and driving them back once more he turned and bolted. At 6 p.m. the farm fell: just forty-one escaped with Baring. Wheatley came to in a ditch beside the body of Ompteda, 'his head stretched back with his mouth open, and a hole in his throat. A Frenchman's arm across my leg.'

With La Haye Sainte captured, roar of battle was now behind Wheatley – already a prisoner. 95th light companies, out-flanked and forced back from the knoll to main line, came under intense fire. French even had two guns in farm back garden, only 250 yards from Wellington's command post. 95th's rifle fire halted cuirassiers, who themselves retreated, 'stooping and stabbing at our wounded ... men's lives were held very cheap there,' thought Kincaid. Now, near 95th, began 'one continued blaze of musketry' between lines only eighty yards apart, with smoke so thick men could see nothing but 'flashes of the pieces'. On the left, Leach glimpsed French officers time and again wave their infantry upright and advance some yards before a storm of fire drove them back. For next two hours the duel raged, 'closest and most protracted almost ever witnessed'. Exposed crossroads area was a death trap, swept by grape from French guns brought on to knoll barely 100 yards away, while whole line was riddled with musketry from hordes of tirailleurs crawling closer. Wellington had brought in Lambert's Brigade from east; 27th Inniskillings relieved 32nd, formed square immediately behind crossroads as a barrier to cavalry threat down Genappe highway, now wide open. 27th endured worse fire than any other unit in the army,

with men falling in swathes, losing two-thirds of its strength by day's end. Kempt's Brigade was still beside Lambert's; at one time their Piper patrolled outside the 79th's square, playing 'Cogaidh na Sith' to encourage the Highlanders. The Rifles were almost at breaking point when again the blue-coated figure of the Duke rode up behind; again the firm voice rose above the uproar: 'Stand fast, 95th – we must not be beat – what will they say in England?'

Musketry and gunfire was so close and heavy that balls were striking Mont St Jean farm, where Simmons lay, 700 yards behind the crossroads. Surgeons were tiring, saws blunting, with lines of wounded still awaiting amputation. Simmons's body so swollen he could hardly breathe, 'warm blood was still oozing from my side into my trousers, the ends of the broken ribs gave me excruciating pain'. Recognizing a surgeon he gasped, 'Old fellow I am hard hit at last,' and touched the lump in his breast. Once the nearly flattened ball was cut out, a gush of clotted blood brought some relief. Stray shots were bringing a shower of dust from the roof when someone came shouting that they must run: 'It is all up with us.' In the rush even 'poor fellows who had lost a leg ... crawling like crabs', until only Simmons and another officer, Lt Stillwell, were left, unable to move. Stillwell, tears down his face, took his friend's hand, 'our race is nearly run ... beaten, beaten ... the French will soon give us a taste of the cold steel.' Simmons managed to speak: '... I never loved you half so well as I do at this moment.'

Whole of Alten's Division, in the centre, was almost destroyed. Macready watched two French guns, protected by cavalry, unlimber 'within seventy paces ... their first discharge blew seven men into the centre of the square'. Unable to charge for cavalry, his regiment simply closed gaps. Macready felt 'the first frenzy of fight' all gone; battle now a grim duel to see 'which side ... could stand killing longest'. Several times the 'murmur of "silence – stand to your front – here's the Duke"' steadied the ranks; once while Wellington was passing the rear face 'a shell fell among our Grenadiers and he checked his horse to see its effect – some men were blown to pieces ... he merely stirred the rein of his charger apparently as little concerned with their fate as his own danger.'

Such appalling casualties could not go on for ever. Halkett, fearing complete collapse, finally sent to ask if his brigade could be relieved; but Wellington had no front line troops near, and sent back the aide. 'Tell him what he proposes is impossible. He, I, and every Englishman in the field, must die on the spot which we now occupy.'

Wellington was by now nearing the west end of the ridge. Whole French divisions were acting as skirmishers, light 6 pdr guns close behind, pushing back Allied gunners. He ordered units from Maitland's and Adam's Brigades to extend in four deep line to drive them back, then reform in the face of cavalry.

But although flanks held, Halkett's Brigade was breaking; Ompteda's sacrificed, Alten and Prince of Orange both wounded.

Shaw Kennedy, senior staff officer now, brought the news of impending disaster to Wellington, beyond the Nivelles road. The Duke sounded cool, determined, almost prepared. Dispatching Kennedy to round up 'all the German troops of the

division ... and all the guns' he could find, he promised Brunswickers and others from reserves behind the Guards. As Wellington himself led these troops up he could see from thick smoke over Plancenoit that Prussians were in action there, suggesting other Prussian columns must surely be near on the Ohain road. The central crisis was so serious he sent aides to order in British light cavalry from the flanks.

Vivian got the order just as he was about to move anyway; already hundreds of figures were visible streaming back from the smoke-shrouded ridge. From the other direction, horsemen in blue were suddenly coming down the road from the east. As a patrol set off to check they were indeed Prussian, bugles called the brigade into column of threes. Passing behind Vandeleur's Light Dragoons, partly sheltered in a hollow, they rode towards the battle storm. In the wilderness behind Pack, Lambert, Kempt, things looked so desperate that Ingilby, riding with Gardiner's Troop, R.H.A., assumed they were to shield a general retreat. Crossing the stricken Genappe road, its paving all 'torn up and scattered' by shell fire, Col. Murray, leading 18th Hussars, heard Vivian ask Somerset '"Where is your Brigade?" "Here," said Lord Edward ... mutilated horses wandered or turned in circles. The noise was deafening ... ruin and desolation ... prevailed wherever the eye could reach ...'

Uxbridge, in Hussar uniform on a troop horse, came up and asked Vivian if he could charge. Vivian thought a charge through the wall of smoke ahead would simply mean men losing contact, becoming lost. Uxbridge 'then dismounted ... advanced himself on foot ... down the hill, hoping to be able to see under the smoke', but returned saying Vivian had better keep his brigade back, but formed ready for instant action.

Ahead and to the right, Brunswick reserves had hardly taken post with Nassau troops to plug the centre when a furious burst of fire signalled an all-out effort by tirailleurs and light guns to break through. When 18th Hussars reached the front Murray

found 'troops with white caps' falling back, and beside them
Brunswickers also running; but lines of Hussars closed up to
block the way and Wellington managed to lead back the
infantry.

Beside Uxbridge now, Wellington received the report that
Prussians were at last approaching on the Ohain road. Hours
late, but they might yet be in time ... He wrote an urgent appeal
for '3,000 men to supply our losses'. One staff officer had had
his horse killed; another, Col. Fremantle, rode away with the
note. Leaving the inferno he met Ziethen's staff group, but
Ziethen said he could not detach a part of 'the whole army' now
coming up. While Fremantle tried to argue, gunfire suddenly
swelled to the south; half a mile away French in swarms were
driving towards the village of Papelotte. From a nearby hill,
Muffling saw the incredible: the Prussian advance guard
around Fremantle, anxiously awaited for hours, was turning
round, backing away. Spurring madly, he galloped up to and
through the confusion, to hear that streams of wounded seen
in Wellington's left rear had been thought a general retreat.
Muffling, senior to Ziethen, countermanded orders and himself
led two gun batteries on to a hill while Ziethen swept into
Papelotte.

Vandeleur's Light Dragoons were behind main line now,
themselves closing ranks to stop fleeing Dutch-Belgians.
'That's right; keep them up,' Tomkinson heard Wellington
crying. Other British cavalry were making charges. 15th
Hussars repeatedly, against lancers, but down to half-strength:
Dalrymple carried off with foot hanging by 'a mere thread'.
Lt Doherty of the 13th watched General Hill waving en-
couragement: 'At them, my old friends ...' Exhausted horses
could scarcely walk. At last pressure slackened; first near
Hougoumont, then all along the ridge French infantry were
falling back.

18

LA GARDE – END OF A LEGEND

From the Allied position stretched huge processions of wounded. Simmons, lifted by a soldier on to a stray horse, was borne away fainting from pain, 'the motion ... made the blood pump out, and the bones cut the flesh to a jelly'. Inside the farm, Surgeon Gibney helped in Dalrymple, 'many ... dying', crazed by thirst.

At the front almost a lull; no musketry now, only the ever-lasting French cannonade. Rifles were cleaned, flints renewed, cartridge boxes stacked, ammunition wagons driven up; gunners returned to usable guns. Skirmish line again down littered fields. Adam's Brigade ordered back from forward squares to main line. Wellington himself ordered the 2/95th: 'Unfix your swords, left face, and extend yourselves once more, and we shall soon have them over the other hill.' Somehow, almost unbelievably, the battered line was still intact.

Wellington could not believe battle was ended. For one thing, no one had seen the famed Imperial Guard – traditionally kept back by Napoleon for a final hammer stroke. Attacks so far had been by mainly infantry, or mainly cavalry; next might be both combined. Banking that in any event French cavalry was now too weak to attack again on its own, he rode east from Hougoumont forming all infantry in four deep lines, lying down behind crest, as a compromise formation. French batteries slowed their firing; the lull became a pause.

Through the clearing smoke an isolated horseman was seen churning up the slope, waving a white kerchief and shouting *'Vive le Roi! Vive le Roi!'* He was allowed through the skirmish line, through the 52nd, and up to Colborne. He was dressed as a Colonel of Cuirassiers. Panting and pointing excitedly, he warned of a new attack forming: 'Napoleon is there with the Guard!' Frazer heard him, unsure whether the man was a genuine deserter or not, but took him to Adam, who passed the message straight to the Duke.

The news was true. Napoleon had seen the second Prussian advance, and knew he was now fighting on two fronts. Neither infantry nor cavalry had broken the crest; from now on time and numbers were against him. The odds had shortened since morning . . .

But throughout its career, in battle after battle, the 'Immortals' had never failed. Once certain just where the English lay, 'I shall march straight at them with my Old Guard,' he had boasted at breakfast. In any case, the only other alternative was retreat, which with an army so weakened would spell disaster, his own end. Perhaps he had premonitions: the westering sun, glowing low and veiled, could itself be a symbol, setting on Imperial dreams.

Once more he refused reality, ordering the lie to be spread that the blue columns to the east were not Ziethen's, but Grouchy's. And the *Garde* would attack. Leaving a rearguard rallying point at Rosomme, seven other battalions, 550 men each, in one massive column on a two company front, sixty men wide, would spearhead an advance by every soldier, foot and mounted, in the army. D'Erlon's Corps – what was left of it – on the right; Reille's Corps against Hougoumont on the left; Guard Artillery beside the column and cavalry in support. He, the Emperor, would lead.

With smoke thickening over the Paris wood there was not a moment to lose. Drums beating, the carefully dressed lines moved off beside the Mont St Jean road.

Along the Allied position, the lull was over; clouds of musket puffs were spreading along the hollows where French skirmishers were pushing furiously forward. French batteries were roaring in a faster rhythm. 52nd, like all Adam's Brigade, was ranged in four lines, with Leeke unable to see anything over the crest forty yards in front; shot and shell were just clearing some wounded curled under blankets under the lee of a three-foot bank. Two men stumbled back, each holding an all but severed arm. A dead kitten lay near; to the left, the silhouettes of horses, floundering with legs shot off, nibbling rye; everywhere the smell of trampled grain and gunpowder.

Wellington, riding past Bolton's Battery, asked who commanded, and warned 'the French will soon be upon him'. He galloped as far as the crossroads checking dispositions, then back down the whole line. Minutes later Leeke saw him, for the first time today, 'quite alone' speaking to Colborne, both watching southwards from the saddle, the Duke looking 'very cool' before he turned towards Maitland's Guards.

From time to time the dark mass of the column could be distinguished moving through the valley; it had begun to separate into a wide fan of battalions; later glimpses showed them combined again into two main columns, the larger to the west. French batteries were firing even faster. The beat of drums now, steadily more distinct. Through a rift ascending columns reappeared within close gun range, and within seconds every British and German battery on the central ridge went into action. Bolton's Battery opened with case at 200 yards; Lt Pringle saw the French column 'waving . . . like standing corn blown by the wind'. Capt. Sinclair's guns, further east, so

blinded by smoke they were simply aiming 'over the dead bodies of some horses in front'. Infantry lying behind the guns could hear now. Leeke's blood chilled at the 'rum dum, the rum dum, the rumadum dumadum, dum dum' of the drums, at the hoarse cries of *'Vive l'Empereur!'*

Wellington had stationed himself behind the Brigade of Guards, where it seemed the main blow would fall. On each side stretched lines of red-coats, half buried in corn, silent except for men when hit. This was the first time British firepower had met Napoleon's veterans; would Wellington's weakened lines hold? Sitting his horse amid the hail of shot, all he could do was to wait during the last anxious moments.

Garde artillery was in action now, stirring the blizzard on the crest to new fury. Capt. Shakespeare, Vivian's A.D.C., even leaning forward close to the general's ear, could only make himself heard by bellowing. Closing up gaps as they were torn away, Napoleon's *Garde* tramped stolidly on. Tall, bony men, with 'black moustachios, gigantic caps ... depravity, indifference and bloodthirstiness ... burnt in their faces ... more dreadful-looking fellows ... I had never seen,' thought Haydon the summer before. Every man conscious he had been handpicked, one of the *élite*, disliked yet admired by the whole army. Napoleon had been left behind, sheltering in a quarry: Ney, his fifth horse shot under him, was leading on foot. Past skirmish lines, past the rows of dead, past guns – deserted now – up the last slippery slope.

On the crest, gunfire suddenly stopped. A fractional pause, then Wellington saw advancing lines of grey. Lt Powell, of 1st

Guards: 'as the smoke cleared away a most superb sight opened on us. A close Column of Grenadiers (about seventies in front) ... ascending the rise *au pas de charge ...*'

Wellington's voice roared 'Now, Maitland! Now is your time!' Alone on horseback, he judged the narrowing range: sixty yards, fifty, forty.

Again the resonant voice. 'Stand up, Guards! Make ready!'

Ensign Dirom, on his feet, had a glimpse of 'ported arms, the officers ... in front waving their swords', the column coming as steadily 'as if at a field day'.

'Fire!' Eight hundred muskets, from all two front ranks of Guards, flamed in one volley. While front reloaded, rear ranks fired. To Powell it seemed the whole column 'suddenly' stopped; Dirom: 'staggered ... convulsed'. More than 300 were down.

But French were replying, trying to deploy to a flank to extend their fire power, men stumbling over fallen; only front ranks halted. Colborne, from his position on right, saw the whole side of the column exposed, momentarily in disorder. Taking an instant decision, he sent one company forward, firing; then all of 52nd 'in quick time'. Once past the fog-veiled crest Leeke heard 'three tremendous British cheers', then 'right shoulders forward' came down the line, and the whole regiment, the strongest in Wellington's army, over 1,000 men, was wheeling to its left to face the side of the French. Leeke saw French skirmishers extending outwards, saw the ripple of

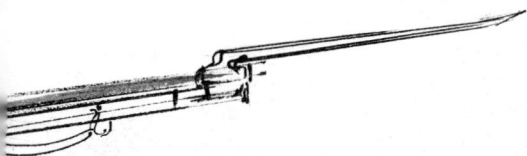

muskets and men around him falling, and then the 52nd was firing at the walk, volley after volley, front reloading while rear two ranks marched through.

Eastwards, a second French column struck the crest by Halkett's pitifully thin line. 'Step by step' the French rose over the skyline, gigantic looking figures with 'high hairy caps and long red feathers' nodding to the beat of a drum. 'Now for clawing,' whispered Macready; already he felt the chill of a bayonet; praying silently that 'it might not touch my vitals'. Halkett tried to make himself heard. 'My boys, you have done everything I could have wished and more ... but much remains ...' French halted; volleys crashed at forty yards; then British lowered bayonets and charged, only to fall under intense shelling from advanced French batteries.

Two right-hand regiments suddenly gave way and recoiled through 30th and 73rd, reducing whole brigade to a mob of running men, with wounded, terrified of being abandoned, clinging hold. A tremendous shout halted the flood; a captain led Morris and a dozen others forward, but half were shot within seven paces. As they lay, pinned by fire, a staff major heard Wellington's 'See what's wrong there', and rode to Halkett just as the general fell, shot through the mouth. 33rd's colonel was near panic, asking for orders. A sergeant of 73rd reported all officers killed or wounded. Kelly took over, and in dense fog held remnants of his old regiment in position against 'noise and clashing of arms' of advancing, invisible French; officers 'cheering their men on'.

Now whole wave had reached the crest. 2/95th, ordered forward by Wellington, was pouring fire into the right flank of largest column, 52nd into its left. To its front, Col. Saltoun roared, 'Now's the time, my boys.' And all at once the Brigade of Guards was charging downhill with the bayonet. Gronow noted the fury of men suddenly released from the torment of standing, seeming to 'single out their victims': French 'paralysed', almost helpless. One huge Welshman felled or bayoneted twelve. Medieval savagery surged and spread, in wild minutes of firing, thrusting, clubbing, stabbing.

Bearing the colour, Leeke was marching in centre of 52nd. Chalmers, cap on sword, 'standing up in his stirrups'; Adam behind; Colborne, shot off horse, wiping his mouth; 'Winterbottom ... brought ... through the line, the blood streaming down ...' Men were falling all around, but ahead of Leeke figures were beginning to run. From rear of dense, packed columns French were throwing down arms, ranks breaking, men fleeing.

Slowly at first, then faster, disintegration swept whole battalions until, suddenly but unmistakably, the grand assault was over. Unable to move forward, outflanked and trapped on three sides before they could deploy, blasted from a position they had thought empty, for the first time in their history the 'Immortals' had failed, formations dissolving into panic-stricken fugitives.

All across the valley amazed French witnessed the incredible; the agonized cry '*La Garde recule!*' spread like wildfire, joined now by a fresh alarm, that not Grouchy but Prussians were coming in from the right.

Everything happening at once. Under swelling gunfire Ziethen's and Pirch's Corps were going into action along lower Ohain road as well as by Papelotte. East of Genappe road, beyond furthest *Garde* column, a skirmisher ran into 92nd saying 'something extraordinary' was going on in the French lines. Through a telescope Sgt Robertson made out troops in blue firing on the French flank; the Adjutant thought it might be mutiny; then an A.D.C. came galloping and crying 'The day is our own – the Prussians have arrived.' Men were frantic to charge now; 'only by force' N.C.O.s kept them back.

Watching his guns firing steadily, Mercer was 'singing out, "Beautiful! Beautiful!"' when someone seized his waving arm,

saying quietly, 'Take care, or you'll strike the Duke,' and
Wellington, 'looking serious ... much fatigued' told him to
cease fire, and rode on. Then 'a line of infantry ... slowly, with
ported arms ... ankle-deep in ... mud' panted up the reverse
slope with feeble hurrahs, paused near Mercer to regroup, and
passed on into smoke, towards the French.

Wellington met Uxbridge; although Uxbridge worried at
a premature advance, Wellington was convinced the whole
French army was finished. 'Oh damn it, in for a penny, in for a
pound is my maxim, and if the troops advance they shall go
as far as they can.' Rising to full height in stirrups, deliberately,
three times, he waved his hat in a high forward sweep. Within
seconds, news of the signal spread to the whole field.

Kincaid, just beyond crossroads with 95th, blinded in hanging smoke, had walked to each flank, 'but nothing met my eye
except the mangled remains of men and horses...' As fog began
to lift, Harry Smith, from Lambert's staff, saw 'the red coats in
the centre, as stiff as rocks ...' Then 'a cheer' which Kincaid
knew 'to be British, commenced far to the right ...' Smith rode
to meet Wellington, 'galloping furiously to the left'. 'Who
commands here? ... get into a column of companies of battalions, and move on immediately.' Smith asked where. 'Right

ahead, to be sure.' Kincaid heard the cheer 'growing louder ...
we took it up by instinct ...' Men were cheering Wellington
now. 'No cheering, my lads, but forward, and complete your
victory!'

Wellington met Muffling returning. 'You see Macdonell has
held Hougoumont!' he cried. Both turned to gaze back for a
moment. Muffling: 'small masses of only some hundred men,
at great intervals were ... everywhere advancing', leaving
behind a red line 'as far as the eye could reach' of uniforms of
fallen. High on the crest, Frazer had never seen or would see
anything 'like that moment, the sky literally darkened with
smoke, the sun just going down ... the indescribable shouts of
thousands ...'

19

VALLEY OF DEATH

On lower slopes French were far from beaten. Many Guards and other infantry were forming squares, cavalry defence lines, guns still firing. Capt. Churchill, aide to General Hill, leading up six squadrons of light cavalry to 'a general charge', spotted the red-headed Ney. He was 'within twenty paces' of a Marshal of France, almost alone. 'I holloaed out to our rascals, but nothing could get them to face him.' His horse, shot through, trapped him below it; cuirassiers counter charged, rode over him until he made off on a riderless mount, but Ney escaped.

Vivian's Brigade was charging now. Vivian led up 10th Hussars against cuirassiers and lancers; 'having seen them fairly in', he rushed back for 18th. 10th at full gallop overthrew lancers, Taylor's 'men cutting in among them'. 18th, clattering across Genappe road to French east flank, took some guns, found French cavalry retreating and infantry broken, but some Imperial Guard units fighting boldly. The 18th's Colonel Murray was nearly bayoneted; his orderly cut 'down five or six in rapid succession...'

52nd, plunging way beyond the line of Hougoumont woods, came under more battery fire; a company charged the guns; an explosion left Leeke with blackened thumb and colour pole dripping red, but himself unhurt. 200 yards from Genappe road they were reforming lines when Wellington rode up: 'Never mind, *go* on, Colborne, *go* on! They won't stand. Don't give them time to rally!' and 52nd charged again, driving French past now deserted guns, right up to paved road.

Cavalry still pressing. Uxbridge exchanged his horse for one from 23rd Light Dragoons, but no sooner had he joined Wellington than a cannon ball passed through the body of his horse to smash his knee. The cavalry commander was carried off in blankets. Wellington was urged to back out of intense fire, but was too full of thoughts of victory to worry now. 'I'll be satisfied when I see those fellows go,' he insisted.

Nothing short of a miracle kept him unharmed. Hunter Blair, sent by General Adam to see if more French cavalry was coming up from south, found one staff officer left behind the Duke, a Sardinian speaking French: *'Monsieur, je ne parle pas un seul mot d'anglais.'*

All British cavalry were on the move. Tomkinson's squadron, riding through wounded and ruin, passed Col. Canning, shot and propped on knapsack, who refused all help, telling Tomkinson 'it was quite useless'; they rode nearly as far as Rossomme before two guns fired 'a few round shot'. Orders were going to everyone to join the general advance. A staff colonel found Col. Muter, 'helmet beaten in ... arm ... in a sling', at head of survivors of Union Brigade, 'many wounded, with bandages, standing by their horses'. Giving the aide one unforgettable look, Muter summoned his men, who managed to break 'into a sort of canter'.

Mercer was firing over heads of men advancing into the valley. Guns were strained to their limits: in Bolton's Battery one burst loaded with shrapnel, severely wounding Col. Napier. Mercer's Battery had fired no less than 700 rounds per gun, an average of two each minute for six hours. Suddenly 'a black speck' caught his eye, with a 'whush' brushed past his collar point and smashed into a horse behind him. Another shell burst

at his feet. His whole battery was under new fire from the left. Forcing around trails his exhausted gunners tried to reply, but drivers, horses, guns were suffering worse destruction now than all day. A Brunswick officer shouted that they were firing on Prussians; Mercer, astonished, pointed angrily to his own casualties, saying he would stop when the Prussians did. Only when Belgian guns mistakenly opened up at point blank range on the Prussian battery, driving them off, did Mercer's men gain a respite. At last gunfire along the crest died, as main struggle receded into the distance. An aide galloped up 'shouting ... with all his might, "Forward, Sir! Forward! It is of the utmost importance that this movement should be supported by artillery."' Mercer merely pointed to his ruined troop, all 'in one confused heap, the trails crossing...' and quietly asked, 'How, Sir?'

In gathering dusk, all infantry advancing behind cavalry: ahead only grenadiers of Napoleon's Imperial Guard formed squares by *La Belle Alliance*, trying to make a rallying point for French army.

Well behind the lines now, Wheatley, pockets rifled and epaulettes stripped, menaced, jeered at, had been taken back under guard as far as Genappe. He entered the town alongside an infantryman propped on horseback; the man's leg, attached by 'one single piece of sinew' where the knee had been, 'dangled backwards and forwards splashing his horse with gore ... the fellow pale and aghast, chewing dry biscuit...' *'Voilà, un français!'* said an officer proudly. Everywhere the ruin of battle. Against a wall a man shot sideways through the head with 'both his eyeballs hanging on his cheeks ... mouth ... open', blood oozing from his ears and fluid from the empty sockets. 'Nothing could equal the horror of his situation.' Under a tree some British horseguards; one groaning, 'Oh Sir, I'm cut all to pieces. Both of my collar bones are divided.' Another, half-disembowelled.

After some minutes Wheatley was marched on southwards, while the sound of gunfire grew fainter. An officer stopped a drunken cuirassier from killing him. A farm woman threatened him, 'Ah, dog!' but his guard silenced her.

As night drew in over the battlefield, last slow charges were pushed home, often over 'bodies ... lying so close ... horses could scarcely advance without trampling on them'. Many in Capt. Barton's 12th Light Dragoons 'wounded in the fetlocks from the bayonets and other weapons' littering the slope. One dense square of the *Garde*, too strong to charge, 'literally walked from the field in a most majestic manner'. In last fighting around Rossomme, however, Taylor was among French units hopelessly mingled, helmets and uniforms of all kinds, 'Imperial Guard, blue with large fur caps ... throwing down their arms ... roaring *pardon* ...' Another line, 'infantry with cavalry behind' formed on a hill, but it broke and ran. Beyond a last deep hollow a solid square, black against the sky, did stand; and British Light Cavalry was called off. Taylor's horse Chopin was 'quite done, and could barely make a walk back'. A single shell burst near. 'It was then moonlight ...'

Tomkinson's Light Dragoons had charged, broken, cut down party after party of enemy; were now fired on from huts built by French reserves on a hill behind Le Caillou. French retreated again, but with light completely gone, 'being ten o'clock ...' said Tomkinson, 'the brigade was ordered to retire'.

Unable to see targets, gunners were standing by cooling pieces. Capt. Walcott R.H.A. was sent to collect all Horse Artillery casualty lists. Infantry going into bivouac where they could. Morris's 73rd retiring right back 'to about fifty yards of the spot we had been fighting on all day'. Adam's Brigade dropped at furthest tide of advance; Tom, with 71st, 'charged right through' a village 'killing great numbers ... formed on the other side ... and lay down under the canopy of heaven, hungry and wearied to death'.

Leeke's 52nd had gone furthest, sweeping way past *La Belle Alliance*, surprising many French in a cutting near Rossomme, and had halted by some abandoned knapsacks of Imperial Guard. The colour sergeant offered Leeke some bread from one: 'I'm sure you deserve it, Sir!' Leeke felt proud and flattered. Officers gathered around a fire; the roll was called and casualties noted; scarce water was shared. In near darkness bodies of Prussians were marching past. One officer asked Leeke in French if the colour was British; he patted him on the back with a '*Brave anglais.*' A Prussian band serenaded them, playing the British anthem in slow time.

Jackson, as staff officer, had ridden east to speed approaching Prussian cavalry; returning, he was following advance. Past wrecked wagons, past rows of French muskets gleaming in the light of a blazing barn and laid down 'in quite regular order' near Rossomme, he overtook Prussian infantry streaming in from the east 'bayoneting every wounded Frenchman they came upon'. He saved one dragoon just in time, '*Er ist ein Engländer.*' He found Wellington with Colborne, saying something about sending up flour for the men. The Duke then headed back for Waterloo, 'followed by five persons only'. Near *La Belle Alliance* again, Jackson heard cheering, and saw

a group of horsemen approaching across the fields. It was Blücher and staff. He saw the two leaders halt, lean from their horses, grasping hands, but was too far away to hear Blücher's breathless greeting: *'Mein lieber Kamerad!'* Then, in halting French, *'Quelle affaire!'*

Wellington and Blücher, and their staffs, agreed that the enemy must not be given a moment to regroup; but the Prussians alone would continue the advance. The British could barely drag themselves another yard, and already the Allies had exchanged fire. Having to use the common language of French made confusion by night too risky.

Gneisenau, slow to move before, began a relentless non-stop pursuit. In an ecstasy of revenge, with the bare excuse of no spare men to guard prisoners, French were cut down and slaughtered in droves. Through the hours ahead, each time they managed to form, drummers on horseback sounded the charge, Uhlans and Hussars advanced as if supported by infantry, and the French stumbled away from imaginary attack. Given no rest, more and more deserted, or collapsed to be killed.

Narrow Genappe bridge was a death trap, blocking up thousands in the town; men too panic-stricken to filter out through fields or to ford the shallow river, some even shooting

and stabbing each other in desperation to get through the
jam of wagons; ruthlessly slashed down by pursuing cavalry.
Napoleon's coach itself was stuck, with the Emperor inside.
Wildly planning new armies, a stand before Paris, for the
moment he was intent only on escape. The coach was captured
seconds after he leapt to a horse and took to the fields.

In battle area, only mopping up left. 92nd was bivouacked
near *La Belle Alliance* farm, where men found a well to quench
their raging thirst; only next day discovering it was filled with
dead. Gronow, looking inside at what had been one of
Napoleon's headquarters, found remains of bedsteads and
chairs over the embers of an 'immense fire'. In the yard, hacked
cows and pigs. All along the Genappe road, cottages ransacked,
doors torn off, wounded murdered in wake of Prussians.
Tomkinson's squadron stopped near woods thick with fugitives, but it was too dark to pursue. Troops dropped where
they stood.

Some – old soldiers like Lawrence – still able to think of
food. The 40th needed fuel; one man, Rouse, set about an
enemy powder wagon with a billhook, struck a spark on a
hidden nail, was blown skywards and lay blinded, cursing,

every stitch of clothing burnt off, to die later 'raving mad'. In
Hougoumont fires smouldered; Wheeler, bivouacking in the
orchard, wandered to the yard: 'What a sight ... Guards lay
in heaps', also charred bodies, 'legs burnt to a cinder' while
trying to crawl free. Clay tried to cook the rest of his pig's
head among the embers of what had been a barn; found the
flames were from a corpse. The scorched pork tasted worse
than before, but in a corner, smothered in brick dust, a pot
of porridge was still warm.

Nearby, Morris had been out binding wounds as long as daylight lasted. Everyone was suffering 'intolerable thirst' from salt provisions, from dehydration following bleeding, calling for water. Morris's ears, roaring from day-long cannon fire, remained deaf for three days, mercifully unable to hear 'the cries and shrieks'. Along Mont St Jean road, Ingilby, sent from Gardiner's Troop of Horse Artillery to collect ammunition wagons, could scarcely move for those who had crawled in from the slopes; some already crushed by retreating artillery.

When a 'sombre and dejected' Wellington and silent staff rode slowly into Waterloo 'the village clock had struck ten'. Following at a respectful distance, Jackson found standing room for his horse and entered the main room of the inn, noisy with foreigners.

One Dutch staff officer, shovelling food, was boasting loudly of his exploits, of leading cavalry charges. Wearying of drawing him on to ever wilder claims, Jackson went upstairs to find some rest. He was allotted a room booked for Delancey, now wounded, but was met by deep groans. His candle showed a booted, burly figure, a French officer, begging for help from the bed. *'Regardez, monsieur'* – he pointed feebly to a gash out of his skull. Blood was everywhere. He told Jackson no one had been near for hours. As the Englishman bathed the wound and got him soup, he related the news of French defeat. The Frenchman took it philosophically. 'Ah well, we've had our victories...'

In another room, Frazer sat writing. '11 p.m. ... so tired that I can hardly hold my pen ... all now ... is confused ... In this very house are poor Lloyd (leg shot off but not yet amputated), Dumaresque ... dying; Macdonald, Robe, Whinyates, Strangways and Baynes, wounded ... What a strange letter is this ...' Along the passage, Wellington had given his bed to friend and aide, Col. Gordon, and lay on a mattress. Surgeon Hume had amputated the shattered leg, and given Gordon 'laudanum with a little antimonial wine' against the pain.

Surgeons were working through the night; as Gordon grew calmer, Hume operated on Uxbridge. Wiseman, of Uxbridge's own regiment, couldn't bear to watch: '... he never moved or complained; no one even held his hand. He said once ... he thought the instrument was not very sharp.' Bearing it stoically to the end, he managed a smile: 'I have had a pretty long run, I have been a beau these forty-seven years ...'

Later, he greeted one visitor almost nonchalantly. 'Vivian, take a look at that leg, and tell me what you think of it.' After gruesome inspection, Vivian agreed it could not have been saved.

In the street outside, carts of wounded were crawling towards Brussels. For miles north, all the way to Namur Gate, one nightmare blockage: no shelling now, but littered equipment, wagons without drivers, walking wounded, men lying collapsed. Hope, shot during last attack, was carried through earlier: 'Without legs, without arms, soldiers ... crying for help ... begging to be placed on a wagon ...' Rumour of defeat had sent hundreds stumbling into Soignes forest; wild stories flew north through the traffic; more wounded crawled from carts to die in the woods.

Simmons, through his agony, saw Brussels citizens 'with flambeaux in their hands'. His legs were so swollen he couldn't move; a mattress on a high table was brought from his old billet; he was 'eased bodily out of the saddle' on to it 'and carried back to the quarter I had left only four days before ... now a ... helpless creature'. In the main square the wounded were stretched on straw, without surgery. Throughout the night the rumble of wagons continued as more and more were brought in.

Almost everyone in the capital believed by now the battle was lost. The English visitor Creevey had seen two great batches of French prisoners earlier, but reports grew more alarming all evening. Between 10 and 11 p.m., a wounded major assured him there was 'no time to lose', and offered to commandeer a carriage; but Creevey and family decided to stay on rather than risk confusion on the road by night.

A whole countryside was on the move. South of Waterloo, Wheatley was dragged on through the French retreat. Resting with two guards on a pile of dung, he was stripped of boots and stockings, then prodded onwards, mile after mile, the stones cutting his feet. By Fleurus they passed a plain strewn with Prussian corpses from fighting three days ago, now stripped naked; in places so thick he got relief from 'treading on through soft jellied lumps of inanimate flesh'. Under a moon almost full, the French staggered south; horsemen cloaking their armour, everyone swearing; Wheatley himself so parched he tried a puddle but retched horse urine.

Somewhere ahead, Napoleon with a group of officers stood staring into the night; but whether his vision was of hope or despair no one knew.

20

FIELDS OF DESOLATION

All over the field of battle, unwounded survivors prepared for sleep. Mercer's men too exhausted to move: smoke-blackened, 'spattered with mud and blood', seated on trails, stretched beside guns. Voice gone, deafened, like everyone with a raging thirst, Mercer crawled on a wagon footboard, out of sight of the carnage around his troop.

Some strange bedfellows. Two men seeking a brother from the 52nd lost their bearings and sheltered in a barn beside two armed French, who gratefully offered themselves prisoners. Keppel laid his head on a tree root by Hougoumont's gates. Up the hillside Clay slept snug in his blanket next to a comrade half-blinded by a powder flash. Macready's last waking thoughts: will 'the day's work . . . be called an action or a battle?'

Morris was up at midnight, craving water. Unable to face the surrounding horrors, he was turning back, when he thought he heard a voice. A man was 'sitting upright' against a horse's belly; but going to lift him his hand 'passed through the body': it was only a shattered corpse held together by its uniform.

Many men were exhausted beyond rest. Tom, in 71st, twitched all night, refighting his battle in nightmares. Mercer was up, under scudding clouds and a pale moon, walking a field strangely still. 'Here and there some poor wretch' trying to staunch his life's blood; some crawling and dropping; horses with 'entrails hanging out' trying to rise, again and again, as long as they had strength; everywhere 'melancholy neighing'. Near him Prussians were bivouacked; dark stern men with 'drooping moustaches', eating and smoking, watching him in silence.

In hollows, banks, ditches; wherever they had fallen or crawled, men lay dead or dying. One staff captain with his head against the neck of his wounded horse. Col. Ponsonby, of 12th Light Dragoons, with so many lance gashes it was a miracle he survived. Shaw had fought his last fight; speared and shot, he had dragged himself to the main road, whispered to a wounded comrade, 'my side is torn by a shell'; at dawn found dead 'with his cheek in his hand'.

On the floor of the noisy common-room in Waterloo's inn, Jackson was awakened from an 'appalling dream' of imminent death, by Col. Torrens shaking his leg. Handing him a sheet of paper, Torrens told him he was to 'act as a sort of whipper-in' for all units.

'*Memorandum*. The troops belonging to the Allied army will move upon Nivelles at daylight. (signed) Wellington.'

Upstairs, Hume was taking a casualty list of officers to the Duke. As he read out name after name the surgeon saw tears among 'the dust and sweat' on his commander's unwashed face. As dawn broke, Wellington pulled himself to a table and wearily began his official dispatch.

'To Earl Bathurst,

My Lord,

Bonaparte having collected the 1st, 2nd, 3rd, 4th and 6th Corps of the French Army, and the Imperial Guards, and nearly all the cavalry, on the Sambre...'

Restrained words spread slowly across the page.

By now Jackson was on his way, past dark ruins, riding as in a dream. But gaping holes in the walls of La Haye Sainte proved yesterday was all too real. A grey dawn showed the desolation: 'every vestige of crops had disappeared, the ground looking like a vast fallow'. Everywhere wreck and litter; in a road cutting beyond the farm a huge smash of 'guns and tumbrils packed and wedged together', many having toppled down the 10-foot banks. Under the trees by Hougoumont, remains of 33rd and 69th lay in one huddled unit. Sometimes little shelters of blankets screening a senior officer, not yet carried away. Regiments accepted the order grumbling – many still without food – but prepared to march. Only the Cumberland Hussars, who yesterday deserted the field for Soignes forest, point blank refused.

French had had no rest at all. When Wheatley limped into Charleroi at 'morning twilight' his two guards fell dead to the world. An Imperial Guardsman squatted beside him, and asked for a 'recommendation' in a notebook for use should he be captured himself. Wheatley took the pencil, and wrote, 'I, Edmund Wheatley ... write this on a bundle of bricks, June 19th 1815...' asking for better treatment than he had received.

Someone gave him a drink; there was sudden commotion as Napoleon rode through, bodyguard 'with drawn swords'; and he was hustled away. Some soldiers tried to force him to the dragropes of a cannon, tied his wrists to a horse tail when he refused, dragging him until he fainted.

A cuirassier 'of immense stature' took pity, and put him behind his saddle: for two hours the Englishman rode with hands clasped around the cuirass; then he was put down and a two-franc piece thrust in his hand.

As day lightened over Mont St Jean, horrors grew clearer. To Tomkinson, riding up from the south, the whole crest looked not so much like an extended battlefield as 'a breach carried by assault'. Frazer later told Mercer a great tidemark, a 'dark mass' of bodies, marked the position of his guns. Even soldiers were sickened. Robertson amid 'bodies ... not scattered ... but ... lying in heaps...' By 6 a.m. 92nd had men out carrying the wounded to the roadside to wait for wagons. Gronow took his shako, bullet hole stopped with his kerchief, dripping from a ditch among men almost mad from thirst. The only sign of life from exhausted 33rd and 69th were burial parties. Mercer's men asked if they might bury Hammond first; the eyes, left in a flap of face without a head, had seemed to follow them all night. 'He looks frightful, Sir ...' Mercer, like many officers, toured a part of the field. By Charleroi road 'a whole regiment of British Infantry fast asleep ... wrapped in their blankets ... in regular ranks, with their officers and sergeants in their places...'

Other strange sights. Capt. Ross Lewin of 1/32nd, riding a replacement horse from the collection of captured animals in the artillery park, saw 'a dead Highlander lying on his back, with his arms firmly bent in an exact boxing attitude'. Nearby, a dragoon with hands as if in prayer. Keppel, wandering with others, returned alone, too depressed, especially by 'the body of a boy who ... could not have been more than fourteen

years of age', stripped naked, with fair hair and tiny white hands; perhaps a German volunteer.

Some food was about. Grove, without a bite for seventy-two hours, was called over to 7th Hussars, where a slice of pigeon pie and brandy 'made a new man of me'. Leeke even frying beefsteaks. Daylight gave men more heart to gather, to ask about friends, to feel their luck in being alive. An explosion suddenly interrupted: two men from 95th followed the path of the 40th; chopping an ammunition wagon they too struck a spark. Kincaid turned to see them 'twenty or thirty feet up', then falling to the ground, by 'some extraordinary effect of nature ... spring ... five or six times, to the height of eight or ten feet, just as a fish does...' Burnt black and naked, but alive for a while.

Among the grain and mud, disregarded yet, thousands and thousands of diaries and letters, fluttering and trampled. Some men, mostly officers, were already writing a note home to catch the wagons before they marched. Capt. Bowles, of Cold-stream Guards: 'just time to tell you my head is on my shoulders...' Natty Staff Col. Gomm: '...we shall be in Paris as fast as our legs can carry us. Tell Aunt so, and recommend her to leave off croaking ... I have been four days without washing face or hands, but am in hourly expectation of my lavender water etc...'

At 7 a.m., the thinned ranks of 92nd, 186 men out of 588, began their march. Hearts heavy at so many comrades unburied: Robertson said he wept.

Waterloo had become another battlefield, sorting order from chaos. Forty-eight spring wagons just in from commissary supply depot were halted by Wellington, and reserved for carrying wounded. Frazer had asked about captured guns: a harassed Sir George Wood, commanding all artillery, admitted he knew nothing. After a fruitless search, Wood braced himself to tell the Duke. So many solid trophies simply missing drove Wellington 'into a towering passion, frightening poor Sir George out of his wits ... swearing by God the guns must be found,' wrote Jackson. They were later traced to Genappe, mostly with British chalk marks, under Prussian guard. An artillery captain, arguing hard, got half the number released; but poor Wood wrote the day after: 'My sun is set ... having received the most severe reprimand before the whole of his Staff and Servants...'

Weather had cleared after Saturday's storms: Wellington set out for Brussels under a bright sky. Working his way through the crowds, silently eyeing the confusion and wreckage, his feelings were numbed; conscious thoughts all on the thousand details ahead, on the unfinished dispatch which would give Britain and the world knowledge of the extent of the victory.

In Brussels, Creevey had first heard the news about 6 a.m., from a Marquis who had it from General Alten – brought in wounded late at night. At 11 a.m., Creevey joined the crowds around Wellington's house in the Park. Seeing his old friend the Duke 'alone at his window', Creevey managed to catch his eye, and was beckoned up. Brushing aside objections from General Hill, Creevey raced upstairs to offer congratulations; Wellington, perhaps as a temporary release, seemed happy to talk 'in his short, natural, blunt way', but 'without the least approach to anything like triumph or joy'. Walking up and down, he praised the Guards, the courage of the French, of all the troops. 'It has been a damned serious business ... the nearest run thing you ever saw in your life...'

By hot midday, the unmistakable smell of decomposition began to taint the air for miles around Mont St Jean. Officers were taking last walks over the field. Gronow estimated 2,000 dead in Hougoumont orchard alone, dappled in the shade of splintered apple trees hanging like willows. Mercer had finished devouring some veal from wagons at last come in, when his first visitor arrived. A gentleman alighted from a coach, a 'perfumed handkerchief to his nose', stepping delicately to avoid soiling his stockings against the corpses, but soon retreated under the sullen stare of the gunners. Mercer walked to Hougoumont garden, 'suddenly and unexpectedly ... in solitude, pacing a green avenue'. Birds were singing; dead guardsmen lay half-hidden among cabbages and turnip tops. No stench rose here: only the sweet smell of turf. Walking on, he came across a French lancer, who with one hand severed gestured bravely with the other, telling Mercer the French were

amazed at the ferocity of the fighting; they had been told the British would put up only a 'token' resistance. Back at his troop, Mercer set to work reorganizing: horses rounded up, fresh harness stripped from dead ones, badly wounded animals shot, ammunition counted.

The slopes were covered now with other figures. From miles around, peasants were flocking like crows to take revenge. After cottages, livestock, crops ravaged by three vast armies, they were out for anything they could get. Tomkinson caught one pulling the boots from a guardsman still alive, and thrashed him with the flat of his sword. Mercer, revolted, joined a German dragoon in driving away some so moronic they thought to curry favour with the victors by kicking and abusing a French corpse. French wounded were terrified at being left to their mercies, even imploring to be killed first. 'They looked on us as brother soldiers,' said Mercer. In ditches, in hidden folds of ground, knives were out, murder easy...

Loot between soldiers was another matter. Before marching, 52nd held a sale; Leeke bought two brass pistols. Tomkinson discovered 'excellent French watches' going for a song.

Both Lambert's Brigade and Mercer's Troop were off by 3 p.m. The Nivelles road shimmered for miles with the arms of plodding, still exhausted men. But with horrors behind them, spirits rose: in Keppel's regiment, resilient youngsters were decked out as cuirassiers, in helmets, in hussar hats. Jackson was kept busy until afternoon, patrolling roads filled with stragglers seeking units, deserters routed out from Soignes

wood, fresh supplies – all branching right at Mont St Jean. Corpses even there lay thick; one with head crushed flat by passing wheels, still in the village street.

After a bite at Waterloo Inn, Jackson rode back to army base in Brussels. In the disordered city, panic was over and citizens were bringing food and help to the wounded. One Sergeant heard a young girl's gentle voice, as she moved his kilt to bandage a Highlander, 'Me no ashamed ... indeed, I will not hurt you.'

By evening, troops were drawing in to the carnival atmosphere of Nivelles; its coffee rooms packed with 'every nation under heaven'. The word 'Waterloo' still almost unknown: fourteen-year-old Ensign Short wrote his mother, 'The name of the place I do not know, but you will see it in the Gazette, and it will be remembered by Europe as long as Europe is Europe.'

21

WOUNDED AND BURIALS

With Tuesday, last excitement forgotten: across battle slopes only misery greeted another day's scorching sun. Hay, sent back at midday to round up stragglers, found the road glittering with so many cuirasses it seemed 'paved with steel'. Corpses were swelling; with dearth of carts every ditch filled with wounded. In Waterloo he picked his way through baggage and dense crowds to a 'wretched cottage at the end of the village' to see a friend from Scottish days, Col. Delancey. His young wife pointed to the bed where, under a coat, her husband of two weeks lay 'with just a spark of life left'. Still dusty from her journey from Antwerp, she gave Hay 'some wine in an old broken teacup...' There was little he could do. 'I bade her farewell...'

Wellington came, and doctors and other visitors, but she never left the cottage until Delancey died in her arms a week later.

In Brussels all churches were taken; almost every other house a hospital. Surgery was simple: wine or spirits for warmth; amputation or probing; sewing up, plugging with lint, bandages kept moist; and, last and always, bleeding. Many men, having half bled to death on the battlefield, were drained unconscious and killed by ignorance. Simmons, deathly weak after six quarts taken in four days, starved on toast, was tortured two more weeks with leeches, before the abscess burst and 'the matter flowed forth as from a fountain. I was immediately rational', fever suddenly gone. Against orders, he smuggled in 'porter and beefsteaks', and never looked back.

Wounded were being brought in all 20th and 21st, French last of all. Almost all French refused help from Royalist surgeons, chanting '*Vive l'Empereur*' in 'a kind of song' until they died. 'They had no King but one', wrote Hope. Juana, wife of Harry Smith, was one of hundreds seeking husbands. Riding in from Antwerp on horseback and told he was killed, she galloped to Mont St Jean, inquiring among the wounded, desperately searching among the bodies, before she learnt it was a Smythe, not Smith, who had died. She reached Mons by midnight, Bavay the next day; at last reunited.

All Tuesday the advance continued. Leeke's unit as far as Binche, where in holiday mood he went sightseeing, 1,100 feet down a coalmine. Mercer, doomed to be left always without orders, following his nose, forcing through traffic jams as if 'to some great fair' towards Nivelles. With guns blocked for hours, he found the town one huge party, cabaret windows wide, men 'drinking, swearing, singing and smoking', citizens doing the trade of their lives. A column of prisoners in grey passed, laughingly returning insults about their 'bastard' Emperor.

By Wednesday, conditions were critical for those still alive in the open, suffering hunger, thirst, gangrene. Stench of putrefaction rose even stronger with a third day's heat. Hay, returning from Brussels, found it 'insufferable'. Nothing deterred plunder; practically all corpses were picked clean, bare of every stitch, until they gleamed like pebbles among the rubbish. Prussian patrols were out 'shooting their own and the French wounded' who were beyond hope. Humanitarian help from a populous countryside hardly existed. One eye-witness thought many kept clear of wounded from fear of being pressed into burial parties. Square holes, six feet deep, each took thirty to forty bloated bodies, loose earth forked over. Corpses were plundered until the end. Some 'Russian Jews ... chiselling at their teeth' with hammers for gold fillings. The occasional crack of pistols, as horses were shot. Sometimes in a final frenzy an animal started up and careered and plunged, menacing last helpless wounded.

Most dismal memorials were hidden in Soignes forest. As late as 31st July, an English tourist, James Simpson, travelled the graveyard of those who died on the road back, 'the mounds ... every hundred yards ... hoofs, and even limbs, frequently appearing. Often bayonet scabbards stuck out; and caps, shoes, and pieces of cloth, scarcely in the gloom distinguishable from the mud ...'

22

*S*OUTH TO PARIS

News of victory spread. At dawn on the 19th, Highlanders bringing their wounded were shouting it through Antwerp. By noon a staff colonel, Henry Percy, was rolling through the Brussels gate on the eighty-mile journey to Ghent, Bruges and Ostend with a copy of the battle dispatch in his wallet and two French eagles sticking out of the windows. A twenty-four-hour ride through muddy roads, embarkation Tuesday, Wednesday stranded by calms off Broadstairs, a long haul ashore by row-boat then a hired post-chaise galloping the Canterbury and Rochester road all afternoon and evening, a breathless dash through the crowds and up the steps of 44 Grosvenor Square towards midnight, and the whole Cabinet, assembled for dinner, read the astounding news. An hour later, as streets overflowed, Percy, still in battle-stained jacket, almost dead from fatigue, lay the eagles at the feet of the Regent in a ballroom in St James's Square.

The next morning, the 22nd, the *Gazette* was out, *The Times* printed a second edition, and London went mad. Haydon read it 'the last thing before going to bed. I dreamed of it and was fighting all night; I got up in a steam ... and read the *Gazette* again ... called at a confectioner's and read all the papers till I was faint.' The shock of Napoleon's downfall – the Emperor was his idol – sent the writer William Hazlitt into a drunken stupor, 'unwashed, unshaved', for weeks on end; but when he finally recovered it had cured him of alcohol for ever.

Napoleon reached Paris on the 22nd to rally support, failed completely, and abdicated in favour of his son. Brussels saw the painful transport north to Antwerp, bargeload by bargeload, of less serious wounded, while in hotel rooms and apartments men died or slowly mended. Amputations went on for days. Costello watched a veteran dragoon holding one sawn-off arm with his other, clenching a plug of tobacco, suddenly rise up to a Frenchman who was screaming under the forceps to beat him with the severed limb, shouting, 'Take that, and stuff it down your throat, and stop your damned bellowing!'

As the army's siege guns were landed alongside the Brussels canal, packed lines of pursuit stretched south. On Wednesday, outside Mauberge, Mercer saw a column of the 92nd break ranks to mob the passing Greys, cheering, clasping hands, blocking the road; that evening he crossed the frontier in rain to the cheers of French civilians. Thursday he was fighting Nassau infantry trying to force his guns off the road in Bavay forest; all Friday through hills and romantic glades; halted at Cateau headquarters on Saturday to let rear units catch up. Keppel limped in starving and was recognized by the Commandant: 'Holloa, youngster ... what can I do for you?' 'Give me something to eat,' he gasped, and was treated to a slap-up meal. Wheatley had escaped, lying up twenty-three hours behind a wall, and after four days' wandering reached Mons, staggering in arm-in-arm with a wounded Scots Greys trooper.

The same day Mitchell's Brigade stormed Cambrai, meeting little resistance. Wheeler's friends were in liquor again, 'picking up some money in the town'. One drunken party opened a

barrel with a pistol; being a powder keg it exploded and killed four, two more than had died in the assault. On Sunday the 25th 'His pottle belly Majesty', Louis XVIII, entered Cambrai, and while British troops ringed the city greeted his 'loyal citizens'. 'Louis blubbered over them like a big girl for her bread and butter, called them his children, told them . . . about his heart, and about their hearts, how he had always remembered them in his prayers . . .' Soldiers like Wheeler who admired Napoleon despised 'an old bloated poltroon'.

Mercer, with the advance, was travelling side roads, through endless wheatlands, and on Monday hundreds of smallholdings, where people had never heard of Wellington, or Louis, or even Napoleon's surname Bonaparte. Tuesday he forded the Somme. This second week, under hotter skies, the pace slowed, and he savoured hard-boiled eggs on horseback in the cool of the morning.

Prussians were always ahead, south and eastwards, never seen. Grouchy, after a day-long battle at Wavre while Waterloo was lost, had retreated south, fighting two more defensive battles, but was forced into Paris. Blücher wanted total surrender, the Emperor hanged, and France bled white. Two more French armies laid down arms. As Napoleon reached Rochefort harbour on 3 July, French outposts before the capital were swapping brandy with Hay's dragoons. On the 4th the city surrendered and Prussians marched in.

No triumph left behind them. As the two armies' paths converged, Mercer found the roadway 'covered with rags, feathers', smashed chests of drawers by defaced walls, villages empty, crops abandoned. He came nearest to death in the whole campaign from a huge mirror, 'launched over the bannisters above' by Prussians ransacking a château, crashing inches from his head. The place belonged to Jerome Bonaparte, but it was only one of many in ruins. At last Mercer was among unspoiled gardens with figs, and people living normal lives, and beyond Argenteuil he had a country house as billet: with guns on the lawn, books of spicy engravings in the library, a cellar of wine and a butler to serve, he was 'in heaven'.

Forestalling trouble, Wellington kept British troops outside Paris, assigning them a huge camp area in the Bois de Boulogne. Only single regiments mounted daily guard in the Champs Elysées; even officers needed a pass. But nothing could spoil the holiday mood. 'Our tents is quite a set off,' wrote Wheeler. 'The Parisians flocks out of the city, so that we are amused with thousands of visitors ... We have ... every kind of vegetable and fruit ... the brandy is tenpence a quart, the old campaigners in my section has not been to sleep.'

Through the trees the roofs of Paris, hidden from Europe for two generations, shone like magnets. Wheeler gaped one day through the Louvre and Tuileries, 'never in my life did enjoy a more rich treat'.

Tom felt more homesick than he had for years when two girls, running up on the first day's parade, turned out to be Scottish – working in Paris at embroidery. 'We're Paisley lasses,' they cried; 'this is our regiment; we want to see if there's ony body here we ken.' Even the toughest Glasgow hearts melted.

Wellington became half administrator, half politician. British sentries foiled Blücher's savage attempt to have two bridges, Jena and Austerlitz, blown up; but it was British and Austrian troops who escorted the return of European art treasures Napoleon had brought home as trophies: Tintorettos,

Titians, and, under the eyes of a screaming mob, the famous bronze horses from St Mark's in Venice.

Although under foreign soldiers, Paris continued almost unchanged. Officers with money had the time of their lives. Gronow found its boulevards and salons his spiritual home; Mercer's artistic eye was aflame – but amused to note 'Imperial' everywhere repainted to 'Royal', even the triumphal 'N' chiselled away from stonework. At a grand review on 24 July the British army showed its paces; admiring Parisians couldn't credit that the infantry who had defeated their Imperial Guard looked so small.

Life in the Bois was divided between parades, carousals, domestic chores; a sham fight near St Denis enlivened October. Sgt Lawrence, old campaigner, fell at last, shot by Cupid, hostage to a pretty fruit-seller by the gates. The colonel reluctantly allowed that she at least 'would do to teach the soldiers French', the parson was called, and the couple moved to a married hut.

Amid balls and gaiety, Wellington enforced the strictest ban on pillage: V Division was fined £5,000 for allegedly ruining a village, although Mercer believed it never paid. Blücher, schemes of revenge blocked, with diplomats taking over from soldiers, haunted the gaming tables, suddenly a morose old man. For some weeks Wellington ordered troops to help with the harvest. French farm lads resented the red-coats' pull with their girls, but in the shadowy evenings loaded carts rolled back amicably enough, nations side by side.

Little joy was left for those in Brussels. By October Simmons was well enough to visit a friend who had lost his leg. Dressed in 'Rifle jacket to receive me ... he took off his night cap and gave *three cheers*', but seeing Simmons shocked and silent, broke down: 'Oh George, my career as a soldier is wound up, for ever!'

By Autumn, the army was in winter quarters. Wellington had horses sent, and foxhunted the coverts around Cambrai, his country headquarters. Hay was mothered by a widow who had lost her only son at Waterloo, and given his gun, his jacket, his dogs. Wheeler and mate cheered the kitchen of an old couple whose six sons had all perished in Napoleon's wars; passing the long evenings with 'a good fire and brandy punch ... our host is not such a bad singer...'

By year's end regiments were sailing for England. Wheeler realized he had fallen in love on his next to last night ashore, with 'two devils', daughters in his billet in Boulogne. Too late, he dreamed of 'Janette'; on 2 January he landed at Dover. Waterloo men were fêted. People of Rye treated every returning regiment to 'a quart of eightpenny stout' per man; when Morris's 73rd marched through Colchester, with tattered colours with the word 'Waterloo' in gold, the whole town was on the streets.

Back in June, Picton's body had been given a hero's welcome: flags in the Downs fluttered at half-mast as ships passed the news; the coffin was rowed ashore to minute guns, and escorted by all naval and military to lie the night at the Fountain Inn, Canterbury. The most famous grave in Waterloo itself was for Uxbridge's leg; coffined, enshrined by a plaque under a weeping willow, a tourist pull for years.

For many summers cottagers sold mementoes to visitors sightseeing the battlefields. The first Waterloo anniversary, Wheeler's 51st paraded in Brighton. The 10th Hussars filed on the Steyne, a bugler sounded 'Prepare for cavalry', square was formed 'in an instant' and non-stop volleys of blank cartridges astounded the populace. One of the most sublime sights he ever saw, declared one admirer. Beef and plum duff and 'plenty of brown stout' followed, and 'ladies and gentlemen' drank the soldiers' health.

Wellington, overlord of France while Commander-in-Chief of armies of occupation, was created Prince of Waterloo, voted £200,000 by a joyful Parliament and returned home to enter the Cabinet, to a life of adulation, derision, misunderstanding, and of veneration after his death. He spoke little of battles, almost never of Waterloo, but sometimes with a certain dry affection for his veterans. And he insisted that the Waterloo Medal, when it was struck, should be identical for both officers and men, saying they had equally shared in the danger.

Blücher died on his farm, finding a last pleasure in life breeding horses. Napoleon, denied refuge in Britain, in second, bleaker exile, a thousand miles below the Equator in St Helena, filled empty days dictating memoirs, fabricating a legend.

For soldiers, the Napoleonic adventure was over. Their seven years served, they could sign on for life – like Wheeler – or take their discharge. At the end, the cold eye of the Clerk to a Medical Board, as he recorded a pittance daily pension:

'Wm Billings 45th Ft ... 15 years 257 days service ... age 41 Cause of discharge: *Worn out*. 1/-'
or '14 years ... *Ruptured and bad Sight*. 8d.'

Lawrence's wife marched through France, sailed on the colliers to Leith and, when he eventually got leave, trekked south by his side to Dorset. It was a Sunday when he entered the village of Bryant's Piddle. People were leaving church, his father on sticks now, his mother 'coming along like a spread-eagle with the same old black bonnet ... she had when I left her ... she was so overcome ... I had to lean her up against the house to prevent her falling...' He had been away sixteen years.

After a wild reunion, with brother and sister and beer from the pub, the next day his mother got out all his letters and insisted on reading every one through to him; by nightfall it 'almost sent me crazy. I advised her to burn the lot...' After the high skies of America and Spain the sleepy village seemed cramped, and his wife was more tearful than he when leave was over. But the roving life ended when much of the army was disbanded; he became a labourer, publican, widower to an old age in Studland.

Tom was disbanded in Flanders. It was ten years since he had last seen Leith, but it seemed only 'the day before' that he had boarded the transport for the Isle of Wight to join the 71st. Now he thought people would recognize him and jeer; with burning cheeks he slunk into Edinburgh by the Easter

Road. A stranger answered his knock; his father was dead and his mother, very ill, had moved. Bad times following the war threw thousands like Tom out of work. For fourteen months he tended his mother; after her death he bequeathed his story to a friend. He finished:

'I would be useful, but can get nothing to do ... I will go to South America. Or, I shall go to Spain, and live in Boho, – I will go to Buenos Ayres – Farewell! John, this is all I have to leave you ... If I succeed in the South, I will return and lay my bones beside my parents: if not, I will never come back.'

The thousands who fought and won that Sunday vanish from view. Some treasured medals remain; some relics of clothing or badges; for most, a name and a line in a muster roll their only memorial.

INDEX

SOURCES AND ACKNOWLEDGEMENTS

Manuscript Sources

British Library (MSS), for originals of Waterloo Letters, and for Lt Duperier.

National Army Museum, for journals, diaries, letters of Bakewell, Black, Dalrymple, Elton, Gordon, Grove, Macready, Murray, Oldfield, Ponsonby, Pritchard, Shakespeare, Short, Simmons, Somerset, Wheeler, Winchester.

Public Record Office, Kew, for War Office in and out letters for C. in C., Commissariat, Transport, Medical Board Kilmainham, and Scovell Papers.

Royal Artillery Library, Woolwich, for Dickson Papers, referring to Col. Wood.

Printed Sources

British Library, Colindale, for newspapers.

British Library (State Papers), for Minutes of Evidence on the State of Mendicity in the Metropolis (for vagrants and beggars), 1815.

St Bride's Library, for information on *The Times* and other newspapers.

Victoria Library, for *London Directory*, 1816, for Mails, mail routes and Post Office; this, and *Picture for London* for 1815, by John Feltham, for information generally on London.

Waterloo Letters, edited by H. T. Siborne, for reports by Barnard, Barton, Colborne, Dirom, Elliot, Evans, Graeme, Halkett, Ingilby, Kelly, Kincaid, Mercer, Murray, Muter, O'Grady, Powell, Pringle, Seymour, Standen, Taylor, Tomkinson, Uxbridge, Vandeleur, Vivian, Waymouth, Whinyates, Wyndham, and others not quoted.

Memoirs, etc, mainly in National Army Museum.

Anton: *Retrospect of a Military Life*, by James Anton, 1841

Baring: *History of the K.G.L.* by North Ludlow Beamish, 1832

Blücher: *Hussar General* by Roger Parkinson

Clay: 'Account of Adventures' in *Household Brigade Magazine*, 1958

Creevey: *The Creevey Papers*, edited by John Gore, 1963

D'Arblay (Fanny Burney): *Diaries*, 1854

Delancey: *A week at Waterloo* by Lady Delancey, 1906

Dickson: Account quoted in *With Napoleon at Waterloo*, edited by Bruce Low

Douglas: Accounts of Cols. Campbell and Douglas on Elba in *An Englishman at Home and Abroad* by J. B. Scott, edited by Ethel Mann, 1930

Ellis: Related by Basil Jackson

Ewart: Quoted in *The Waterloo Roll Call* by Dalton, 1890

Frazer: *Letters* by Sir Augustus Frazer, Longmans, 1859

Gibney: *Eighty Years Ago*, edited by R. D. Gibney, 1896

Gomm: *Letters and Journals of Sir William Maynard Gomm*, John Murray, 1881

Gronow: *Reminiscences and Recollections of Capt. Gronow*, 1900

Hay: *Reminiscences 1808–15 under Wellington* by Capt. William Hay, 1901

Haydon: *Correspondence and Table Talk* by Benjamin Robert Haydon, 1876

Hope: *Letters from Portugal, Spain and France* by A British Officer, Edinburgh, 1819

Jackson: *Notes and Reminiscences of a Staff Officer* by Lt-Col. Basil Jackson, John Murray, 1903

James: *Surgeon James's Journal*, edited by Jane Vansittart, Cassell, 1964

Keppel: *Fifty Years of My Life* by George Thomas, Earl of Albemarle, Macmillan, 1876

Kincaid: *Adventures in the Rifle Brigade* by Capt. J. Kincaid, 1830

Lake: In *Scots Guards Magazine*, 1961

Lawrence: *The Autobiography of Sgt William Lawrence*, edited by Nugent Bankes, 1886

Leach: *Rough Sketches of the Life of an Old Soldier* by Lt-Col. J. Leach, 1831

Leeke: *The History of Lord Seaton's Regiment* by the Rev. William Leeke, 1866

Lewis: Quoted in *The Battle of Waterloo* by A Near Observer, 1815

Mercer: *Journal of the Waterloo Campaign* by General Cavalié Mercer, Blackwood, 1870

Morris: *Recollections of Military Service* by Sgt Thomas Morris, 1845

Muffling: *Passages from My Life*, translated by Philip Yorke, 1853

Ompteda: Account in *History of the K. G. L.* by N. L. Beamish, 1832

Picton: *Memoirs of Sir Thomas Picton* by H. B. Robinson, 1836

Robertson: *Diary of Sgt D. Robertson*, quoted by Bruce Low in *With Napoleon at Waterloo*

Ross-Lewin: *Life of a Soldier* by A 'Field Officer', 1834

Shaw-Kennedy: *Notes on the Battle of Waterloo* by Gen. Sir James Shaw-Kennedy, 1865

Simmons: *A British Rifleman* by George Simmons, 1899

Smith: *The Autobiography of Lt-Gen. Sir Harry Smith*, John Murray, 1903

Smith: *The English Army in France* by Surgeon John Gordon Smith, 1831

Tom: *Journal of a Soldier of the 71st or Glasgow Regiment* by Tom S., Edinburgh, 1819

Tomkinson: *Diary of a Cavalry Officer* by Lt-Col. William Tomkinson, Frederick Muller, 1971

Uxbridge: *One-Leg: The Life and Letters of Henry William Paget* by the Marquess of Anglesey, Jonathan Cape, 1961

Verner: Diary quoted in *Long Forgotten Days – Leading to Waterloo* by Ethel M. Richardson, 1928

Wellington: *Dispatches of F. M. the Duke of Wellington*, edited by Lt-Col. J. Gurwood, 1834–9

Wheatley: *The Wheatley Diary* (of Edmund Wheatley), edited by Christopher Hibbert, Longmans, 1964

Wheeler: *The Letters of Private Wheeler*, edited by Capt. Liddell Hart, Michael Joseph, 1951

The author and publishers would like to thank the following for their kind permission to reproduce contemporary prints:

BRITISH MUSEUM (PRINTS), for *Bank of England*, by Shepherd; *Billingsgate*, by Cooke; *Millbank*, lithograph by G. Harley; *London Bridge*, by Cooke; *View of Park Lane*, part of print of Hyde Park, in Crace Collection; *View of St Paul's*, entitled 'St Martins Le Grand', by Thomas Girtin; *Winchester Street, London Wall*, by J. T. Smith; *Belleville*. NATIONAL ARMY MUSEUM, for use of many prints as general reference and for permission to draw uniforms and arms. NATIONAL MARITIME MUSEUM, for *Britannia entering Portsmouth Harbour*, oil painting by George Chambers. TATE GALLERY, for *Rue St Denis*, watercolour by Thomas Girtin. VICTORIA LIBRARY, for *Covent Garden*, part of print by Pugin and Thomas Rowlandson; *Horse Guards from St James's Park*, by Robert Havell; *Lobby of Drury Lane Theatre*. ROYAL ARTILLERY INSTITUTION, WOOLWICH, for permission to draw from lithographs of Royal Carriage Department. VICTORIA AND ALBERT MUSEUM (PRINT ROOM), for *Costumes for 1815*, by Ackerman; *South View of Somerset House*, part of print by Joseph Stadler; *Elba*, detail from series of views by J. R. Cousins; *Transport off North Foreland*, part of watercolour by S. Owen; *Ramsgate from the East Pier Head*, by Ducutes; *View of Royal Naval Hospital, Greenwich*, part of lithograph by Daniell; *Horse Guards*, by Thomas Malton; *London Docks*, by H. Moses; *Mansion House*, by Thomas Malton; *Aquatic Theatre at Sadler's Wells*, dated 1813. BRITISH LIBRARY (MAPS), for Map of Waterloo by Craan, as basis for drawing of plan of battlefield.

In particular, the author wishes to thank the staff of the National Army Museum Library for their very great help and guidance towards his research.